180!
Fascinating
Darts Facts

180!
Fascinating Darts Facts

Patrick Chaplin
Foreword by Sid Waddell

To Maureen

First published 2012

The History Press
The Mill, Brimscombe Port
Stroud, Gloucestershire, GL5 2QG
www.thehistorypress.co.uk

British Library Cataloguing in Publication Data.
A catalogue record for this book is available from the British Library.

ISBN 978 0 7524 8611 6

Typesetting and origination by The History Press
Printed in Great Britain

Contents

Foreword

by Sid Waddell

I t is probably a good idea to lead you into this book about the wonderful world of darts by describing my own journey into the far-flung reaches of the game.

My odyssey started in 1956 when I was a grammar school swot trying to pass exams and get to Oxford or Cambridge University. My relaxation was to play darts in a Northumbrian pub with miners, brickies, wide boys and wastrels. The whole raffish boozy ambience intrigued me; this was a vivid world just like the one in the movies. Everything seemed hyped in the glow round that board and people became actors in mini-dramas. I knew then, and still insist today, that darts is working-class theatre.

And it did not surprise me in 2011 when World Champion Adrian Lewis kissed Prince Harry! The sport is infectious; you can hardly move for top footballers and cricketers enjoying the crack at big events.

Cut to 1960 to a pub in Cambridge and my St John's College team salivating at the prospect of smashing some trainee vicars in the university darts final. Fat chance! We got plastered in more ways than one! Hence one's empathy when Jocky Wilson fell off a stage or a cocky Eric Bristow led with his chin and got whopped. Darts is never far away from drama, be it comic or serious. As Patrick Chaplin tells herein, our sport is a kaleidoscope of colourful emotions projected by volatile characters.

Now we move to the 1972 News of the World Championships on national television and a fiery little Welshman called Alan Evans beating the reigning champion as hundreds of his fans waved red scarves and plastic leeks! The floodgates had opened – a pub pastime was helter-skelter en route to becoming a world sport.

I am delighted to say that darts has fulfilled all my fantasies of where it could go. Phil Taylor has sent averages into the stratosphere and has been hailed by stars in every sport. James Wade left behind his mechanic's spanners in a garage and treads the boards like Robbie Williams. Simon Whitlock has a ponytail longer than Rapunzel's . . .

I could go on about this demi-monde forever. And I reckon I can put the appeal of darts into what has been called a 'Sidism'. 'Darts is a sport where you can show an Eskimo your trusty tungstens which have served you well for donkeys . . . and he could be hammering you with them inside five minutes.'

This book is your guide to a special world, one with a colourful exotic past, a vibrant present and a glorious future. So toe the mark, take aim and get enjoying a cornucopia of life on the oche.

Sid Waddell
May 2012

Introduction

by Doctor Darts

Welcome to my fascinating world of darts facts. Of course there have been many books published about darts, the first dating back to 1936, but you will not have read one quite like this before. Trust me. I'm a doctor.

In *180! Fascinating Darts Facts* I burrow deep into my archive to bring you mind-boggling facts, many of which have never been made available before in book form, while at the same time keeping a sharp eye on what's happening in the world of darts today.

Those only recently introduced to the fabulous sport of darts, those who have been involved with the 'arrers' for more years than they care to remember, the armchair sportsmen and women, top professional and enthusiastic regular darts players and those who play purely for the fun of it, fans who attend darts tournaments to watch their favourites play or simply go just for the crack, to socialise, will all find something of interest in *180!*.

I make no attempt to teach the reader how to play the most popular of indoor pastimes (bar one) . . . I have already done that in my book *The Official Bar Guide to Darts* (2010) although hints and tips from the stars of yesterday and today are featured.

History is my main bag but there is no dry and dreary historical stuff in *180!* – present-day revelations mingle comfortably with tales of the past; years of research being combined with recent events place the history of darts in its modern context. I even explode a few darts myths along the way.

You will be pleased to hear that *180!* is devoid of tedious statistics or lists of tournament wins. Not for me the regurgitation or topping-up of previously published lists of champions. No, *180!* is all about enjoying darts in book form and I sincerely hope that I have achieved that . . . but it's for you to judge. Any errors are my own. I have no one to blame but myself.

Darts is my passion and I hope it's yours too.

GAME ON!

Dr Patrick Chaplin (aka 'Dr Darts')
Essex, 2012

'LAGER-SWILLING FAT GITS' AND OTHER CLICHÉS

Being born of the public bar it was to be expected that from Day One, when darts became popularised on television, saturating our screens and the first 'stars' appeared, it would become the subject of ridicule; a pub game being transported into the realms of a sport? You have to be joking, right?

Until the late 1970s few darts players had been 'famous' except locally or as the winner of the News of the World Individual Darts Championship, the latter being a kind of temporary fame for most. Looking back at the images of the News of the World winners up to, say, 1980, there is not a chubby tummy in sight.

But all that was to change . . .

FAME, FORTUNE AND CURRIES

The newly found wealth and the accompanying fame and hectic lifestyles of the new breed of darts player from the mid-1970s onwards produced exaggerated figures that not even the most voluminous of loose-fitting shirts could hide. To a large extent the players had themselves to blame.

With more money than many players had ever seen in their lives and increasing demands on their time, life in the darts fast lane brought with it the quaffing of copious additional amounts of alcohol. With more eating on-the-run, late night curries especially added even more inches to the already cuddly waistlines, transforming the physical form of these new 'athletes'.

'Lager-swilling fat gits' was a phenomenon created during, primarily, the 1970s which the less-than-sympathetic national media seized on from the start. Darts players have been labelled 'walking beer barrels', 'human ashtrays' and 'brainless, 15-stone bags of burping wind'. Darts has been described as 'the Sport of Slobs' and 'child's play' but even so, at its height, over 10½ million people in the UK engaged in the sport.

COMMENTS AND CLICHÉS

Here is just a small selection of some of the comments and clichés aired in national daily newspapers.

'. . . and there on the boards . . . stand big ugly guys in gaudy shirts with the capacity audience well and truly perched in the palms of their ham-like hands.'

Peter Batt, *Daily Star*, 15 January 1981, Embassy at Jollees

'. . . those doughty men who never lack the stomach for the fight.'

The Times – Sporting Diary, 31 March 1984

'A dashing bunch, these athletes of the arrows. Fag in one hand, pint in the other, they display amazing grace by still contriving to throw.'

The Times, 8 November 1999

Whatever anti-dart journalists and commentators said or did to perpetuate the 'lager-swilling fat git' image, that all pales into insignificance when compared to the impact of one single TV comedy sketch.

FATBELLY AND EVENFATTERBELLY

Although first broadcast over three decades ago, no matter how old a darter you may be, *everyone* it seems has seen the now legendary BBC TV *Not the Nine O'Clock News* darts sketch featuring Dai 'Fatbelly' Gutbucket (Mel Smith) and Griff Rhys Jones as Tony 'Evenfatterbelly' Belcher. The commentator with a distinct Geordie accent was played by Rowan Atkinson.

For those rare few who have never seen it, in the sketch 'Fatbelly' and 'Evenfatterbelly', instead of throwing for double tops, throw for double scotch, treble vodka, etc, until the latter eventually throws up. There are some darts pundits who feel that this single comedy sketch indelibly seared the 'fat belly' image of darts players into the minds of the nation forever, produced as it was of darts' popularity. But then that was *exactly* what *Not the Nine O'Clock News* was all about: parodying current affairs and popular culture.

This single sketch etched the archetypal 'fat git' darts player into the national psyche and nothing, but nothing, it seems will ever shift it.

FITTERBELLY

There are many people within and without darts who believe the sport took two giant, chubby steps backwards when first Andy Fordham (2005) and then Bobby George (2006) appeared on TV's *Celebrity Fit Club*. Many more thought it was great entertainment.

Bobby reported on his time on the programme on his website www.bobbygeorge.com. At the end of the piece is the legend, 'If you would like some more information on fit club Bobby says please ring this number: Eighty nothing, eight nothing, eight f*** all!'

LARD BUTTS

The Times journalist Lynne Truss described darts players as 'lard butts'. However, she did confess that the sport itself had 'a certain amount of beauty' and then spoilt it by adding, '. . . if you don't look too closely at the players.' Then to add insult to insult she referred to Ted 'The Count' Hankey as being of 'the same generation as my dad.' Well Lynne, your dad must have started early as Ted was only 31 at the time.

But not everyone in the journalistic profession was against darts. A *Daily Express* reporter in January 1985, wrote, tongue firmly in cheek, 'As athletes, they are anti-heroes. The First of the Flab to make televised sporting history' but, more positively, in 2002 Dave Kidd, reporting for the *Sun* on the PDC world championship, wrote, 'sumo comparisons are unfair in many cases. Dutchman Roland Scholten is built like a pipe-cleaner and Steve Beaton looks like he would be more at home as a baby-oiled thong-dropper at one of the Circus Tavern's popular ladies' nights.'

New York Times journalist Joshua Robinson hit the nail on the head when he wrote in 2008, 'Darts has been saddled with the image of overweight, beer-swilling Cockneys. But it is precisely these characters . . . who have made darts into a wildly popular television sport.' However, such characters are becoming scarcer every year.

Despite these more positive reactions the 'lager-swilling fat git' image continues to haunt and distort darts despite there being fewer and fewer large darts players.

In today's modern game fitness is essential in order to play consistently well at the highest level. With millions of pounds in prize money, professional darts players cannot allow their game to slip and nowadays fitness is part of most top players' training regimes, some even having their own personal trainers and physios.

THE ORIGINS OF DARTS

For many years the history of our sport was dismissed by writers as being 'lost in the mist of alehouse smoke'. This was basically an excuse for not researching the heritage of darts properly or perhaps not even caring. Here then are the facts.

Darts is one of the oldest established English pub games which since the late 1970s has become one of the most popular indoor sports in the world.

THE THEORIES

In the past a number of theories have been presented about the origins of the game. These have included javelins, crossbow bolts, medieval fighting and hunting dartes and archery. Of these the most likely scenario is that the game has its roots in archery. Glance back to the earliest type of dartboards and you will see that these were concentric targets – miniature forms of the archery target. Moreover, darts is most commonly known in England as 'arrows'. Some would say that these two points alone are sufficient to confirm our sport's heritage. But the truth, and this might hurt Englishmen's feelings, is that the modern game of darts is partly French!

Surprisingly, darts as we know it today, is not as old as you might think. True, darts has been played in inns and alehouses in England for centuries, but not in the standard form that we recognise today.

FAIRGROUNDS AND THE FRENCH CONNECTION

Darts from at least the sixteenth century onwards was mainly played as 'puff and dart' where small darts were puffed through a tube at a numbered target. It was not until the mid-nineteenth century that modern darts began to develop. We have the English fairgrounds to thank for that.

During that period the purpose of the fairground in England was changing from a functional market – selling goods and services at, say, the Mop or Goose Fair – to a leisure experience. Always looking for something new to entertain the punters, showmen began to import wooden 'flechettes' (translation 'little arrows') from France for use as a new throwing sideshow.

The flechettes, which became commonly known as 'French darts', comprised of a combined one-piece wooden barrel and stem with turkey feather flights. Later bands of lead were added around the barrel to increase the weight of each dart. The fairground side stalls featured any number of random dartboard designs.

So, like it or not, darts is not wholly English but a hybrid; part English (the dartboard) and part French (the wooden darts).

DARTS SPREAD

From the popularity of the fairground, and as the showmen toured the English counties, slowly but surely darts found its way into English (and some Welsh) public houses.

So, up until the early part of the twentieth century, darts existed in disparate forms across parts of England. As interest grew, the first organised matches were played but these were only 'in-house' or friendly matches between pubs which were close to each other (the cost of transport was prohibitive at that time).

After the First World War, the first brewery leagues appeared and grew to such an extent that, by 1924, the seeds had been sown for the establishment of a national darts association. The National Darts Association (NDA) was formed in London in 1925, its plan to formally organise darts across England, in the first instance, and then into other parts of the UK.

THE NEWS OF THE WORLD

The News of the World competition, organised by members of the NDA, was established in London in the 1927/28 season and covered only the Metropolitan Area of the capital. Just over 1,000 darts players entered that first tournament. By the end of the 1930s it had expanded to cover, by region, most of England; the total number of entrants into the competition in 1938/39 exceeded 280,000. Up until the Second World War there was no national News of the World tournament.

OUSTING OTHER PUB GAMES

Such was the take-up of darts by the brewers and the dart-playing public that, by the 1930s, it had become a popular national recreation in England and parts of Wales, played by all classes, often ousting existing pubs games such as skittles and rings (indoor quoits). However, the development of darts found some resistance in places like parts of Manchester where even today the smaller Manchester/Log-End board still holds sway in Salford and elsewhere.

THE SECOND WORLD WAR

During the Second World War darts-playing boosted morale in the forces, being played in the officers' mess and prisoner of war camps alike. Towards the end of the war, darts became a standard item in the NAAFI sports pack issued to serving troops and this helped spread the word of darts across the world in many theatres of war.

American soldiers visiting England during the Second World War took darts home with them and generated substantial interest in this 'olde English' game in the US which up until then was little played in that country.

POST-WAR

The News of the World Individual Darts Championship was revived in 1947/48, this time on a 'national basis' (in reality only England and Wales), and continued to be described as 'the championship every dart player wants to win' until the tournament was 'suspended' in 1990. The end of the war also saw the return of the People National Team Championships (first played for in 1938/39).

The original NDA did not survive the war and although a number of attempts were made to introduce another national, controlling agency, nothing firm was realised until 1954 when the *People* newspaper supported the setting up of the National Darts Association of Great Britain (NDAGB).

LOW PROFILE – 1950–72

The 1950s and 1960s were periods when darts maintained a fairly low profile even though levels of participation remained extremely high. During this period and into the early 1970s the NDAGB looked after darts in Britain, being responsible for setting up some of the earliest county darts teams in the early to mid-1950s and introducing a number of major tournaments including those sponsored by NODOR (the famous 'NODOR Fours') and Guinness. The 1960s saw darts on television for the first time since the 1930s.

THE 1970s AND 1980s

It was not until the establishment of the British Darts Organisation (BDO) in 1973 and the introduction of split-screen technology that televised darts really took a hold of Britain and then, it seemed, the rest of the planet. In 1977 the World Darts Federation (WDF) was established to become an umbrella organisation for darts across the globe.

The 1970s and '80s created the first household names, the first darts 'stars' such as Eric Bristow, John Lowe, Maureen Flowers, Alan Evans, Jocky Wilson, Leighton Rees and Cliff Lazarenko to name but a few. The Embassy World Professional Darts Championship was established in 1978, the first winner being the Welshman Leighton Rees.

THE SPLIT

In 1993 the world of darts was rocked by what has become popularly known as 'the split'; a situation whereby sixteen of the top professional darts players broke away from the BDO and joined the World Darts Corporation (WDC), now the Professional Darts Corporation (PDC).

The rest, as they say . . .

CHARACTERS

During the Lakeside World Professional Darts Championships in January 2012, Ted 'The Count' Hankey surprised no one when he announced his intention to leave the BDO and 'defect' to the PDC; his intention having been well telegraphed in the tabloid press.

But it came as a bit of a shock to his fans when Ted also announced that he was not only dispensing with his Dracula cape but had also decided to cease hurling plastic bats into the crowd during his walk-ons. While some traditionalists mourned the fact that Ted was joining the PDC, others sensed the end of an era; the end of *characters*.

Was Ted the last showman of darts?

CHARACTERS OF YORE

In the early days darts characters tended to be defined by natural, inherent eccentric behaviour. For example, back in the 1970s Warwickshire's Bob Baxter liked to dress cowboy style (minus the gun and holster) when he was on the oche. After a county match against Middlesex at Southall, his opponents produced the new BDO rule book which stated that no hats could be worn 'without the prior permission of the BDO appointed Organisers' adding, 'for example, a Sikh would qualify for such permission.'

Bob, a 32-year old car assembly worker from Atherstone, thought the rule 'rather childish' but a BDO official told reporters, 'We made the rule because we wanted to lose the cloth cap image.' Such a decision would have also affected Wales' Dyfri Jones who went on stage at an early home international wearing a bobble hat and a white cardigan.

Jeans and 'skirts made with denim, or corduroy material, which have been fashioned in a "jeans style"' plus 'any form of "track-suit" attire' were also outlawed by the BDO, and this heralded the arrival of the style police. The image-makers were knocking the 'characters' out of the game and effectively repackaging darts. Darts players even began wearing suits! Rod 'The Prince of Style' Harrington was well-known for wearing shirt, tie and black trousers on the oche.

ECCENTRICITY

The 1970s also saw 'character' become more about creative, deliberate eccentric behaviour, for example the outlandish walk-ons created by Bobby George, but often 'character' was associated with players' legendary drinking capabilities before, during and after matches.

The BDO gradually put an end to quaffing beers by any player or match official initially 'whilst engaged in a match played on stage the area covered by television.' This ban was later extended to all major tournaments until smoking was banned in public places by the government beginning in Scotland in 2006 and the rest of the UK in 2007. In addition, disciplinary action was taken against any players misbehaving on and off the oche, that is, anyone who technically brought the sport into disrepute.

All of these rules were working against any players' desire or natural ability to be a 'character' but the greatest element working against frivolity of any kind was and is money; shed loads. There is so much money to be earned, especially in the PDC tournaments, that players have to be at the top of their game *all of the time*. Nowadays players simply cannot afford to mess about on the oche. It costs too much.

They certainly cannot expect to go on stage inebriated and escape retribution. If they do then a drug-testing team waits to greet them backstage after the match. Nowadays the walk-on is the only real demonstration of character on TV and as soon as the music stops the real business begins.

CHARACTERS LIVE ON . . .

Actually, it's not the characters of the game that have changed but the character of the game. Fortunately, the darts-wielding characters are still there but not on our TV screens. The exhibition circuit thrives so fans can witness their favourite pros really letting their hair down and having fun. At major televised tournaments nowadays the 'characters' tend to be among the audience wearing fancy dress and brandishing placards rather than standing on stage tossing tungsten.

WHY 501?

In most major darts competitions players play straight in-double out 501. One of the most popular questions received via www.patrickchaplin. com is 'Why is 501 the standard game of darts?' Some even ask 'Why not 300 or 500?'

The very first games of darts consisted of throwing three darts at either a miniature concentric archery target or a random number board, the highest score with those three darts winning the game. But as skills developed things became a little more sophisticated.

The original '01' game of darts was 301 and was scored on a cribbage board. Cribbage (or more commonly 'crib') is an old English pub card game where scores derived from the value of cards were recorded by pegging holes on a wooden crib board. The cribbage board was (and is) also 'borrowed' for scoring the popular pub game of dominoes.

Back then the landlord of your average hostelry would not have had a blackboard and chalk handy; a slate perhaps for writing up credit, but not for use as a scoreboard. The blackboard and chalk would appear later, but the crib board came first.

Each side of the crib board has two rows of thirty holes and one extra hole at each end. To win the game players have to achieve a given number of circuits of the board (60 holes) plus the one extra hole representing 'home', making 61. Any game played on the crib board has to be a multiple of 60 – plus 1. For example 'twice round' would be 120 (plus 1), 'three times round' 180 (plus 1).

In the early days of modern darts the score, to enable scores to be fairly recorded, was defined as 'five times round' the crib board, that is a total of 300 (60 x 5) plus 1 – 301. At every stage of the game the players could see where they were in terms of score by looking at the crib board. Weight is applied for this theory when the Norfolk Board (an early form of miniature archery target) was played '31-up' and the East End 'Fives' board played '61-up', although the starting score in the latter would have been 305. The connection with dominoes is also evidenced by the fact that during the early twentieth century 'DOMINO!' was often shouted at the completion of a darts game rather than the 'GAME SHOT!' we tend to hear today.

When chalking was introduced as darts became increasingly popular, the versions of the game were extended to anything -01, (501, 601, 701, 1,001, 1,000,001, etc).

Also, if the -01 wasn't there it would make darts terribly boring as good players would just keep hitting 20s. With the -01 it means that players have to move away from the 20 bed – at least for a short while – in order to win the game.

THE NINE-DARTER – THE DART PLAYERS' NIRVANA

To hit a nine-dart perfect game of 501 is every darts players' dream. Like a 147 break in snooker or a hole-in-one in golf, the nine-darter is the best possible 'out'. It is the darts players' Nirvana.

SETTING THE SCENE
AND THE PACE –
PHIL 'THE POWER' TAYLOR

Phil Taylor has become the king of the nine-darter. When he recorded a nine-dart leg of 501 (180, 180, treble 20, treble 19, double 12) in his quarter-final match against England's Chris Mason in the World Matchplay at the Empress Ballroom, Winter Gardens, Blackpool, in August 2002, it was rightly reported in the darts press as being the first-ever nine-darter on live UK television. This was a tremendous and long-awaited achievement for which 'The Power' bagged a £100,000 bonus. He then went on to win the title, beating Canada's John Part, and prize money of £15,000.

However, subsequently, Taylor's fine achievement seems to have become hailed by some as being the very first nine-darter hit 'live' on TV anywhere. To set the record straight this actually happened six months earlier.

THE FIRST NINE-DARTER ON
'LIVE' TELEVISION

It was Sunday 3 February 2002. The occasion was the Dutch Open; the venue the Koningshof Hotel, Veldhoven, Holland. The final was being fought out by two Englishmen, Steve Coote and Shaun Greatbatch. There were 5,000 spectators and the match was being broadcast live by Dutch TV station SBS6.

Steve Coote had won the first set 3–0 but Shaun was 2–0 up in the second. Shaun started the third leg with back-to-back 180s and the crowd fell silent. He then struck his seventh treble 20, then treble 15 and finally double 18! As referee Steve Nicholas calmly announced 'Game shot' the audience went mad and continued to applaud and cheer Shaun for a full 5 minutes or more. This was the first-ever nine-darter on 'live' TV.

After the raucous crowd had calmed down, the game resumed and Shaun went on to take the Dutch Open title 4–2 but by then he had already carved his name forever into the history books and thereafter the Dutch fans in particular dubbed him 'Nine Dart'.

What was Shaun's reward for this historic achievement?

£100,000?

No.

£50,000?

No.

Shaun said, 'I didn't win any money for hitting the nine-darter, although after the event someone phoned in and offered two thousand Euros.'

'OLD STONEFACE' SHOWS THE WAY

But, of course, it was John Lowe back in 1984 who achieved the first televised nine-darter. Professional darters, darts fans and pundits were eagerly anticipating the first perfect game on television and the bookies' favourites were Eric Bristow or Jocky Wilson. They simply didn't see John Lowe coming up on the rails.

On Friday 13 October 1984 during the quarter-final of the MFI World Matchplay at the Fulcrum Centre, Slough, Unicorn-sponsored John made darting history when he hit the first-ever perfect nine-dart game of 501 in a major tournament on television. Keith Deller, his opponent that day, looked on in appreciation and applauded as the ninth dart, double 18, struck home. John, nicknamed 'Old Stoneface', even allowed a broad smile to crack his face as he hit the jackpot – £102,000.

His prize money came from two sources; £100,000 from the organisers (who had wisely insured against the feat being achieved) and £2,000 from the BDO. But it didn't end there . . .

John went on to beat Keith Deller 3–1 in sets to win through to the semi-finals. There he whitewashed Bob Anderson 4–0 and went through to meet and beat his old friend Cliff Lazarenko 5–3 in the final. For winning the title John earned another £12,000 but it *still* wasn't over. John was then awarded another £1,000 for the highest out shot of 161. This made John's total prize money for the weekend a massive £115,000; record prize money that would stand for nearly twenty years. No wonder the hotel he was staying at ran out of champagne! John told the *Guardian* in 2007, 'The bill came to £1,100, a lot of money in those days.'

THE FIRST NINE-DARTER AT THE WORLD CHAMPIONSHIPS

The TV darts fans would have to wait six years before they witnessed another nine-darter on the small screen. It came in the 1990 Embassy World Professional Darts Championship at the Lakeside Country Club, Frimley Green, Surrey, and was achieved by the Singapore-born USA darts master Paul Lim in his second round match against the Republic of Ireland's Jack McKenna. For that Lim received £52,000, twice as much as Phil Taylor would pocket for winning the tournament.

Strangely enough, up to 2012 Lim's achievement at the Lakeside has never been matched despite a plethora of perfect games in the PDC world championships. Alan 'Chuck' Norris came close in the 2012 Lakeside but missed the final double, double 12.

WHAT ABOUT THE LADIES?

As for the ladies, England's Mandy Solomons hit the first-ever nine-darter recorded as achieved by a woman in 1995 during a Greater London Super League match. Playing for Hackney against West Ham, Mandy, playing against Cathy Fox in the second leg, scored 180, 180 then completed the feat with treble 20, treble nineteen, double 12 – game shot.

AND THE EARLIEST EVER RECORDED ANYWHERE?

The earliest recorded perfect game was achieved by Albert Gamble, a former Cheshire county player, on Monday 18 October 1976 at the Finger Post pub in Stockport during a Robinson's Brewery Dart League fixture against the Nicholsons Arms.

Albert, a 56-year-old post office engineer, told reporters, 'I was sixth man on in a seven-a-side and [each man] played just the one leg of 501. After I hit the two 180s everyone came round and it was the quietest I'd ever thrown in. I got treble 17, then treble 18, to leave myself 36. That last double 18 was the hardest dart of my life.'

Despite being witnessed by two club secretaries, two licensees, the two team captains plus an estimated eighty other people present and being properly recorded on the league score sheet which was signed by officials, the folks at *The Guinness Book of Records* turned down the application for formal recognition of Albert's feat. They told him, 'Your records are too fragmented.'

Albert won no money for achieving the perfect game, his only reward being his memories of what happened on that October night in 1976. Interestingly, in the following January £50,000 was up for grabs in the British Open for achieving the darting Nirvana.

AND THE NEXT?

Darters had to wait until February 1981 for the next perfect game when Frank Reader, a super league player from Tonbridge, Kent, hit a nine-darter, 'only the second recorded . . . in the history of the game and the first outside a local league.'

Reader, a 27-year-old panel-beater and sprayer, was playing in the East Grinstead Open Singles (first prize £200). After hitting six consecutive treble 20s he recalled, 'I didn't get the shakes or go slow with those last three darts. They all went in so crisp it was as though they had magnets on them.' The final three-dart 141 out shot was achieved by hitting treble 20, treble 15 and double 18. Reader said, 'The whole place went berserk. I won the match but lost after that.'

Like Albert Gamble nearly five years before, there was no scheduled reward (financial or otherwise) for Frank and his nine-darter. However, the East Grinstead Round Table, organisers of the event, gave Frank £25 as 'a gesture' together with 'two tickets for a John Lowe darts evening' plus two return air tickets to Jersey from British Caledonian.

WHAT ABOUT 501 DOUBLES?

In the doubles format of 501 the earliest example of a nine-darter being achieved is in the 1997 German Open Friday 'warm-up' doubles tournament where Wolfgang Boge and Andreas zum Felde from Hamburg hit the perfect game and received a prize of £400. However, if the purists insist on a 'proper' tournament then fast forward to the 1999 German Open Men's Doubles in Herne-Bochum where, in the third round, Belgian darters Erik Clarys and Tanguy Borra, played a perfect game of nine darts. Erik recalls that he and Tanguy received 'special prize money' of 400 deutschmarks.

WHATEVER NEXT?

In early May 2010 Eric Bristow wrote of the level of darts being achieved by darters on TV and the 'loads of nine-darters' being hit over the previous few weeks. He said, 'I'm waiting for someone to hit two in a TV tournament – that would really raise the bar.'

On 24 May 2010, in the final of the Whyte & Mackay Premier League Darts at the Brighton Centre, Phil Taylor responded to his former mentor's wish by hitting two perfect games (and just missing out on a third) against James Wade.

RAISING THE BAR
STILL FURTHER

John Lowe suggests that with so many nine-darters perhaps it's time to set the bar even higher by increasing the 501 game 'for certain tournaments' to 601 or even 701, achievable in eleven darts and twelve darts respectively. John wrote, 'We'd still be playing the same numbers game, but we'd have moved the finishing post. Surely this has to be seriously considered.'

Pause for thought . . .

NICKNAMES

For many years it has been the norm in darts for players to have a nickname. It has become an element of the persona of the darter that they be called *something*.

But in the past a nickname was something that was bestowed on someone by others; a form of flattery, a substitute, often descriptive, a name given as fun or a term of affection by family or friends. And so it is with darts.

However, many nicknames have been created on the spot by people in darts, either during commentary, or by officials or fellow darts professionals. Because of the *need* to have a nickname some darts players' managers invent a name for them, for example in the case of Denis 'The Heat' Ovens in 2002/3, but men like MC Martin Fitzmaurice, commentators Tony Green and Sid Waddell and darts professional Bobby George are more likely to bestow a moniker on a player than any other.

Here then is small selection of the nicknames of some familiar darters.

JAMIE 'JABBA' CAVEN

Jamie's career in darts goes back to his first major success, winning the Winmau Youth World Masters in 1993. More recently Jamie has been winning PDC pro tour events and in 2012 made the top 20 in the overall PDC Order of Merit and the top 25 in the PDC Pro Tour Order of Merit.

Jamie was nicknamed 'Jabba' in the early noughties by Dave Hayes, a friend of Jamie's during his darts league playing days in Leicester. The nickname has its origins in the fact that Jamie is an insulin-dependent diabetic and has to 'jab' himself four times a day.

In 2011 Jamie recalled, 'A few of us were in Inverness in an event around 12 years ago, when I was 4–1 down in a best of nine-leg match. Dave just came out with it and for a strange reason it inspired me to come back and win 5–4. I then decided that if I was to make it in darts then that would be my nickname.'

MIEKE 'BAMBI' DE BOER

Winner of the 2002 Women's World Darts Trophy, Dutch darts star Mieke de Boer was dubbed 'Bambi' by BDO MC Martin Fitzmaurice. Fitzmaurice recalled in 2004, 'I remember she was 12 years of age, and this little blonde girl came bouncing on stage. I thought she looked like a little Bambi. The following day, in front of 2,500 people, up went a 4ft banner with 'BAMBI' on it, and someone even threw a toy Bambi on stage.'

TONY 'THE VIPER' ECCLES

The 2012 Scottish Open Champion Tony Eccles made his first appearance in the Embassy World Professional Darts Championship in 2002 where he lost in the first round three sets to two to England's Wayne Jones.

Despite this short stay in the competition, commentator Tony Green said that Tony's throwing action looked like 'a python doffing its cap'. Tony also commented that the way in which Tony pulled back his dart and threw looked like a python's head when about to attack.

In search of a nickname Tony and his partner Claire Stainsby decided to go along the 'snake' route and the result was 'The Viper'.

TRINA 'GOLDEN GIRL' GULLIVER

It was BDO Master of Ceremonies Martin Fitzmaurice who dubbed Trina Gulliver 'Golden Girl' because of her amazing success on the oche long before she won the first of her (so far) nine Lakeside Women's World Professional Darts Championships.

The consistency of Trina's strike rate was well demonstrated by the fact that, up until the end of the 2008/09 season, she enjoyed a run of 92 games without defeat playing for the Warwickshire County Ladies 'A' team in the British Inter-Counties Championship (BICC). Sadly, in the first game of the 2009/10 season in October 2009 her record-breaking unbeaten run came to an end when Trina was beaten by Yorkshire's Karen Lawman.

FRANCISCA 'THE DUTCH CROWN' HOENSELAAR

The most successful female Dutch darts player ever, Francis Hoenselaar, decided on her nickname back in 1998 at the time when her own brand of signature darts and flights came on to the market. She said, 'Because I had no nickname (and never had one) and at that time I was the most successful Dutch darts player with many, many titles, we thought "she can wear the Dutch crown".' After 20 years as a top player (including winning the Lakeside Women's Professional Darts Championship title in 2009) it has proved to be an excellent choice.

ADRIAN 'JACKPOT' LEWIS

In 2005 Adrian Lewis hit the headlines and it had nothing to do with darts. While over in Las Vegas playing in the Las Vegas Desert Classic, Adrian thought he would try his luck in the casino. Playing the coin slot machines the winning reel dropped in and he 'won' the dollar equivalent of just over £40,000.

However, his celebrations did not last long as, unfortunately for Adrian, US gaming laws state that players must be 21 years old or over. Adrian was only 20 and despite protestations CCTV footage revealed him clearly playing the machine. 'That's where the nickname "Jackpot" came from!' he explained. 'I can smile about it now but it was a blow at the time!'

The memory of that moment lives on in Adrian's nickname.

PAUL 'THE ASSET' NICHOLSON

Paul Nicholson was in sensational form in 2010 when he stormed through to the quarter-finals of the PDC Ladbrokes.com World Championship and continues to pose a major threat to all of his opponents.

Born in Newcastle, Paul holds Australian nationality and this is why Sid Waddell originally dubbed him 'The Aussie-Geordie'. However, Paul is much better known as 'The Asset', a nickname inspired by the New Zealand darts player Barry Whittaker. Back in May 2008 Paul was playing Barry and there was PDC membership at stake if Paul won.

Paul beat Whittaker, checking out on 142. Afterwards Whittaker told Paul, 'You're a cracking asset for darts.' Now there's an idea!

TONY 'SILVERBACK' O'SHEA

Not looking for a nickname of any kind, 2009 and 2012 Lakeside finalist Tony O'Shea was given one in the mid-1980s by his Cheshire county team-mates, long before he played darts in front of the cameras and thousands of fans.

Back then the Cheshire team travelled to county matches in two buses. Tony recalled, 'In those days we used to moon from the back of the bus at the second bus.' Tony revealed that he has a 'rather hairy bottom' which a guy called Tommy Hunter likened to that of a gorilla. 'From then on,' said Tony, 'everyone called me "Silverback".'

RAYMOND 'BARNEY' VAN BARNEVELD

Another professional darts player with more than one nickname, multi-world darts champion Dutchman Raymond van Barneveld is popularly known as both 'Barney' and 'The Man'.

He was dubbed 'Barney' while still at school, long before he took up the sport that would turn him into a national hero. More recently he has become known as 'The Man' but the source of this nickname is not known.

Hans Willink, co-author of Barney's biography *Barney: The Eye of the Tiger*, says 'I think that the nostalgic Raymond prefers "Barney" and the proud darts player prefers "The Man".'

CO 'MATCHSTICK' STOMPE

In 2004 MC Martin Fitzmaurice admitted that he gave the Netherlands' Co Stompe the nickname 'Matchstick'. Fitzmaurice said, 'He [Stompe] walked into the hospitality room wearing a khaki raincoat and a red woolly hat. He looked like a Swan Vestas match.'

ALAN 'THE ICEMAN' WARRINER-LITTLE

Another cool customer, this former World No. I was given the nickname 'The Iceman' in 1988 by his then manager Tommy Cox just prior to the British Professional Darts Championships. Tommy thought that Alan 'looked cool' when playing.

Alan who, among many titles, won the World Grand Prix in 2001, has been a professional darts player for more than two decades but no longer plays on the Pro Tour. From 1 January 2009 he took up the post of Chief Executive Officer (CEO) of the Professional Darts Players' Association (PDPA). He also currently works for Sky as a TV pundit and co-commentator.

He was called 'Wozza' when he was a kid, which is what most of his closest family and friends still call him. Mind you, he was only Alan Warriner back then; the hyphen and the 'Little' were added when he married his partner Brenda Little in Carlisle in 2005.

JOHN THOMAS 'JOCKY' WILSON

On Saturday 24 March 2012 double world champion darts player died and at that moment one of the stars in the darts firmament went out.

There are those who felt that with first names of 'John Thomas', Wilson was lucky to just be known as 'Jocky' but let's face it what else would you have called this most famous of all Scottish darts players? OK, he was occasionally dubbed 'The Wee Yin' but it was by 'Jocky' that he was popularly known.

Jocky was undoubtedly one of the great characters of the sport. He won the Embassy World Professional Darts Championship twice, in 1982, beating John Lowe 5–3 and in 1989 when he beat Eric Bristow 6–4.

One of the founder members of the WDC (later the PDC) Jocky retired from darts in 1995 and lived as a virtual recluse until his death.

Although it seems compulsory nowadays to have a nickname, one multi-titled darts professional said recently, 'The made-up nicknames that some players have now are ridiculous and not nicknames at all. Some not only sound stupid but also look stupid on the back of their shirts. To me it's actually cringeworthy. For some unknown reason players think they have to have one, as if this is wrestling or something. I'm not against them. I just don't think they fit if they are made up.'

DARTS MYTHOLOGY

EARLY DARTBOARDS WERE MADE OF PIG BRISTLE?

When darts was originally introduced into English public houses, the dartboards were cut from tree trunks – either elm or poplar wood. Wood for fashioning darts targets was easily available and there were many craftsmen who had the skills to convert the log-end of a tree into a dartboard; craftsmen that are still around today although in very limited numbers.

When darts was popularised and formally organised in the 1920s it was the wooden elm board that was the target of choice. However, other materials used to construct dartboards have included rolled, coiled and compressed paper, cork, cardboard, clay, Plasticine® and, in Australia, gum. Enthusiastic hobbyists have also been known to make dartboards from dead matchsticks.

The standard dartboards used in league and tournament play are bristle boards which were patented and originally produced by the

NODOR company in 1932. These revolutionary boards were very expensive by comparison with the then existing wooden dartboards but were easier to maintain; the elm boards needing to be soaked overnight to maintain suppleness whereas the bristle board did not, were easier to use (the bristles closed over the hole when the dart was removed from the board) and were cleaner and longer-lasting.

THE MYTH

Unfortunately one author of a popular darts book in 1938 wrote of the bristle dartboard as being 'A more expensive board . . . made of compressed pig bristles on end, again with the grain, as it were, running through the board. This board will outlive many wooden ones . . .'

When the same book, credited to the same author was revised and updated and republished under a new title in 1981 to capture a piece of the throbbing new darts publications market, the porky 'fact' remained, the author stating 'By way of contrast [to the elm boards] the bristle board, usually made from compressed pig bristles facing end-on, is entirely trouble-free . . .'

There is absolutely no truth in the 'fact' that some early dartboards were made of pig bristle or, as someone else suggested, horsehair. Have you any idea how many of our porky chums (or indeed our equine pals) it would take to construct such a board?

The 'bristle' used is actually sisal, a vegetable material which is also utilised in the manufacture of ropes. Today all major competition boards are 'bristle' dartboards. Since the mid-1970s the British Darts Organisation rules state clearly that only dartboards made from African sisal can be used in that organisation's tournaments. The other main source of sisal for dartboards is China.

DARTEFACTS – FAMOUS FIRSTS

THE FIRST 180

It is impossible to say who scored the first ever maximum 180 in either friendly or tournament darts play. Many years ago *The Guinness Book of Records* revealed that a man named John Reader hit the first ton-eighty at the Highbury Tavern, Sussex, in 1902 but, to date, no primary evidence has been found to back up this claim nor can the venue be traced. Another suggestion, that the first 180 was achieved in a bar in Lanarkshire at the turn of the twentieth century, does not hold water as darts did not arrive in Scotland until the mid-1930s.

On much firmer ground, it can be revealed that the first 180 scored in the inaugural Embassy World Professional Darts Championship at the Heart of the Midlands Nightclub, Nottingham, in 1978 was *not* scored by an Englishman.

In the first match of the first round Eric Bristow (England) played Conrad Daniels (USA), which Conrad won 6–3. There was only one 180 scored in the match and that occurred in the first leg on the fourth throw (darts 10, 11 and 12) and was scored by the American. This maximum left Conrad Daniels an out shot of 45 which he hit to win the leg in 15 darts, with Eric after 12 darts leaving 301.

THE FIRST PRODUCT ENDORSEMENT

Take a look at professional dart players today and you'll find their shirts awash with sponsors' logos. This is indicative of the modern era of darts where sponsorship is of paramount importance, enabling the top and emergent darters to travel the country and the globe in pursuit of ranking and Order of Merit points. It is beholden to professional darts players to recommend, endorse and promote their sponsors' products, goods or services wherever they may be playing, and not playing, darts. The earliest example of product endorsement can be traced back to the early 1930s.

In 1931, when the News of the World darts tournament was a London Metropolitan area-only event, that year's champion was engineer's assistant Tommy Nye. He played out of the Tankerville Arms, Kennington, and beat R. Wright from Hampstead 2–0 in the final. After his victory Nye was approached by the paper darts flight manufacturer Butterfly Brand and asked to endorse their product, the 'Truflit'. Nye agreed and the packaging of the flights for a time thereafter bore a quote from Nye which read, 'I consider they are the best flights I have ever used, they last longer, can be thrown closer, and cannot spread.' Although a single example, Nye's (and darts') involvement with product placement was way ahead of any such promotion in any other sport.

More recently, in 2010, Australian darting superstar Simon 'The Wizard' Whitlock endorsed the sterling work of Russ Strobel who works tirelessly for wheelchair darters. Simon became the Ambassador for Russ' invention, the Wildfire 137 darts frame, a product that enables wheelchair players to play the sport on an equal basis with able-bodied darters. Promotional material blasts a message out loud and clear, 'To give up is un-Australian. We fight. We focus. We achieve.'

'OUR 'ENERY' IS FIRST TO SIGN UP

In November 1974 the former British heavyweight boxer Henry Cooper was the first to sign up to play in the Unicorn World Darts Championship. At a special reception held at London's Press Club, 'Enery signed on as an entrant and was expected to be followed by another 20,000 darts player vying for the title.

FIRST PERFECT GAME ON 'THE ROCK'

The first perfect nine-dart game of 501 hit in a major tournament on the Rock of Gibraltar was achieved by Bristol player Stuart Foale at the Central Hall in the stage semi-finals of the Gibraltar Open against Catalan Jose Escudero on Saturday 15 March 2008.

Even though the Gibraltar Darts Association (GDA) had no special prize to award, they passed the hat around and over £200 was raised which the GDA rounded up to £300. This was then presented to Stuart on stage.

FIRST TO RULE THE OCHE

From the first Embassy World Professional Darts Championship held in 1978 until the 1991 Lakeside World Professional Darts Championship, two men reigned supreme over the oche. Between 1978 and the finals in 1991, a period of 14 years, Eric Bristow or John Lowe (or both) appeared in every final. 'The Crafty Cockney' appeared in nine finals and 'Old Stoneface' eight. On three occasions – 1981, 1985 and 1987 – they met in the final. For the record Eric beat John in 1981 and 1985 while John won in 1987.

During the 1990s and 2000s one man, Phil 'The Power' Taylor, ruled the PDC World Championship with only the occasional interruption. Some argued in those early days that the PDC code had no real strength in depth but, of course, that argument hasn't held water for years.

FIRST GATHERING OF FLIGHT COLLECTORS

The first ever international exchange day for darts flight collectors was held at the Café Wolkshuis, Vilvoorde, Belgium, on 31 August 1986.

The technical name for flight collectors is belopterophilist and flight collecting is increasing in popularity year on year. Belopterophilists collect flights in the same way as other people collect stamps, postcards or coins. Flight collectors use coin albums to both store and exhibit flights, except of course feather and rigid flights.

Flight collecting has enthusiasts across the world, especially in Germany, Holland, USA and Canada. World class 'top flight' flight collector, Freddy Olievier of Belgium, has 'many thousands' of flights in his collection.

FIRST DARTS PLAYER TO BE INCLUDED IN THE DNB

The *Oxford Dictionary of National Biography* (*DNB*) is the prestigious 60+ volume work prepared by Oxford University Press. The *DNB* is a national record currently containing biographies of over 58,000 men and women who died in or before 2008; people who helped shape the history and culture of Britain and beyond.

In 2006 Leighton Rees, the Welsh darts ace and first World Professional Darts Champion who died aged 63 on 8 June 2003, became the first ever darts player to be included in the *DNB*.

THE TOURNAMENT THAT CHANGED DARTS FOREVER

Since the World Darts Council (WDC) established its own World Darts Championship, which commenced on Tuesday 28 December 1993 and ran through to 2 January 1994, darts fans have been in a similar situation to followers of boxing, having the luxury of more than one world championship.

In 2012 arguments ensued about just how much of a 'world' title the Lakeside (formerly the Embassy) World Professional Darts Championship had actually become with the field of thirty-two being only drawn from the UK, the Netherlands and Belgium. But while those arguments continue and the new BDO Board do something about it, it is fitting to travel back to 1978 to that first Embassy, where the modern era of darts really began. Although there were 'world' darts titles that were contested before 1978, it was the Embassy that lit the road for the rest to follow, and follow they did.

NEWS OF THE WORLD BEFORE THE EMBASSY WORLD

Before the formation of the British Darts Organisation in 1973, darts had little or no regular television exposure or national newspaper publicity. Up to that time the News of the World Individual Darts Championship was *the* tournament every darts player wanted to win. But there was no major tournament yet provided that would match the growing number of darts professionals (those who earned their living or part of their living from darts) with top non-professional players from the UK and elsewhere.

All this changed forever in 1978.

THE FIRST EMBASSY

Apart from the darts press, the build-up to the first Embassy World Professional Darts Championship was understated. This may have been because it was 'just darts' and few of the national newspapers, especially the broadsheets, paid darts any attention at all. But history was in the making.

The inaugural Embassy was held at the Heart of the Midlands Night Club, Talbot Street, Nottingham, from 6–10 February and offered 'World Record prize money' of £10,000 with the winner taking away a personal cheque for £3,000. The main sponsor was the tobacco company W.D. & H.O. Wills of Bristol (later part of Imperial Tobacco). Wills had been sponsoring snooker for the previous three years but then turned their attention and their money to darts.

The event was promoted as being given 'the full top sports treatment on television with five days of coverage'. What this meant in effect was that BBC2, which had brought sports such as snooker, crown green bowling and even sheepdog trials into millions of homes, would broadcast *a total of three hours* (180! minutes) of recorded highlights of the darts over the five days of the tournament.

The television commentary was provided by David Vine (who had previously launched a TV series called *Double Top* on the regional Westward TV channel) and Sid Waddell who according to the 1978 programme had, while at Cambridge University, lost a darts final to a team of four trainee vicars! Nowadays with blanket live coverage and red button additional features, three hours seems woefully inadequate. However, it did not feel so at the time. This was only the beginning.

THE PLAYERS

For the first Embassy the BDO had invited sixteen of the top darts players from around the world of which eight were seeded, namely Eric Bristow (England, seeded 1), John Lowe (England, 2), Leighton Rees (Wales, 3), Rab Smith (Scotland, 4), Alan Evans (Wales, 5), Stefan Lord (Sweden, 6), Nicky Virachkul (USA, 7) and Tony Brown (England, 8). The eight unseeded were, in alphabetical order: Barry Atkinson (Australia), Tim Brown (Australia), Pat Clifford (Ireland), Conrad Daniels (USA), Alan

Glazier (England), Kenth Ohlsson (Sweden), Hilyard Rossiter (Canada) and Bobby Semple (Scotland).

For those who wanted to attend the Embassy in person and watch history being made, tickets for the first round (Monday and Tuesday) and the quarter-finals (Wednesday) cost £1.25 each, while for the semi-finals fans were charged £1.50 and for the final on the Friday evening, £1.75. On each night play commenced at 7.00 p.m. and after the darts had finished the well-known comedian George Roper entertained the crowds.

A darts pundit at the time wrote before the tournament, '. . . all those people who thought darts was for middle-aged men wearing cardigans to hide their paunches, will be surprised to see "veterans" in their mid-twenties like [Sweden's] Stefan Lord, and a World Master who is only 21'; the latter being a reference to Eric Bristow who was the red-hot favourite to take the inaugural Embassy title, a young man who had lifted the Winmau World Masters title a few weeks earlier. That same pundit looked back at the 'Good Old Days' and predicted that darts was on such a roll that there would be many 'Good New Days' ahead too.

How right he was.

The scene was set and the oche line was set at 7ft 6in. The format for the first and only time in the entire history of the Embassy/Lakeside was legs rather than sets. The first round and the quarter-finals was the first player to win nine legs, then first to eight legs in the semi-final and first to eleven legs in the final. Lights! Camera! Action! The first Embassy World Professional Darts Championship was underway.

AN 'ARROWING EXPERIENCE

No one believed it when the no. 1 seed and hot favourite Eric Bristow crashed out 6–3 in the first round to American star Conrad Daniels, but it happened. Bristow said much later, 'I honestly believed I couldn't lose. I looked at every invited player and knew I could beat them. It was there for the taking,' adding, 'I lost to an idiot.'

All five other seeds made it through to the quarter-finals. With Bristow out of the tournament the fans were perhaps expecting more surprises but there were none (Daniels being dispatched by Nicky Virachkul the no. 7 seed in the quarter-finals) as the no. 2 seed (John Lowe) and the no. 3 seed (Leighton Rees) reached the final.

THE FINAL

In front of a capacity and relatively noiseless yet enthusiastic crowd, both Wales' Leighton Rees and England's John Lowe played superb darts. With the score at 10 legs to 7 in Leighton's favour and him requiring 100 to take the title, Leighton hit a bullseye with his first dart, then single 10 and then double top with his third dart to lift the title and the roof of the Heart of the Midlands Night Club.

For that triumph Leighton Rees was presented with a cheque for £3,000, the Embassy trophy and the title of Embassy World Professional Darts Champion, 1978. However, it is a relatively unknown fact that this was not the only trophy Leighton picked up that day. He was also awarded the British Airways specially designed Concorde Trophy for a superb ten-dart finish in the quarter-final against his friend and compatriot Alan Evans with scores of 137, 180, 180, 4 game shot.

Darts fans would have to wait until 1990 to see Rees' record beaten when at the Lakeside Country Club Singapore-born USA darts master Paul Lim hit the first ever (and up to 2012 the only) perfect nine-darter recorded in the Embassy/Lakeside World Professional Darts Championship, during his second round match against the Republic of Ireland's Jack McKenna.

BETTING AND SPLITTING

At the time of his victory Leighton Rees told a *Darts World* reporter that he always bet on himself. He said, 'I always have £25 or £50 on myself every time I play.' He also split his £3,000 winners' prize money for the World Championship with his great friend and fellow Welsh darts star Alan Evans. Leighton added, 'We always share the prize if one of us wins a big competition.' This splitting of prize money was fairly general practice in darts back then.

And so, Leighton Rees took the Embassy World Professional title and trophy, his cheque and the Concorde Trophy back to the valleys and while John Lowe would gain revenge the following year, the no. 1 seed, Eric Bristow, would have to wait until 1980 to win his first (of five) Embassy titles.

That is where it all began, but where will it all end?

'THEY'RE TEMPERAMENTALLY UNSUITED TO THE GAME' – LADIES' DARTS

Darts has never been made easy for the ladies.

For years their participation in the sport was hardly ever mentioned in the local press and mentions in the national newspapers were scarcer still. Even so, when news of women's darts did appear it was usually of a derogatory nature. For example, in the 1930s a darts league in South Shields banned women entirely from playing darts on the basis that they were 'Temperamentally unsuited to the game.'

This view that the girls became rather excited when throwing darts was shared by author Rupert Croft-Cooke who, in his 1936 book *Darts*, wrote 'With shrill laughter they throw darts off the board, or with self-congratulation on the board,' adding, 'There are women who play darts. They are few and their merits are usually exaggerated.' But despite these kinds of remarks ladies' leagues were set up during that time by courageous brewers and were very successful.

In the summer of 1977 two ladies lost their appeal against a decision by the committee of the Ivy Leaf Workingmen's Club, Burnhope, County Durham, not to allow them to play darts in the bar. The Equal Opportunities Commission ruled that, as the Ivy Leaf was a private club, the commission was unable to take any action. As a result of statements she made to the press, one of the ladies was banned from ever visiting the club again.

PRIZE MONEY

Prize money in the ladies' game has always been shameful. In April 2012 Phil 'The Power' Taylor stood proudly at the top of the PDC Order of Merit with two-year earnings in prize money of £665,100. The other four members of the top five were doing pretty well too – Adrian Lewis (£549,500), James Wade (£378,400), Gary Anderson (£314,900) and Simon Whitlock (£230,800).

At the Lakeside in 2012, men's champion Christian Kist received a cheque for £100,000 while ladies' champion Anastasia Dobromyslova's reward was £10,000, which was less money than the joint third position players received in the men's tournament. Women can only dream of earning six figures.

The men's game has come on in leaps and bounds whereas clearly the ladies' hasn't. Compare the above earnings with the annual earnings rankings revealed for 1983, where Eric Bristow earned £28,050 and top lady darter Sharon Kemp earned a whopping £2,665!

BIASED PRESS OR JUST NOT INTERESTED?

Coverage in the darts press has always had a bias towards the men's game but that seems to be changing, very gradually, with, for example, one or two of the tabloids listening to what Anastasia Dobromyslova had to say at the 2012 Lakeside World Championships. Multi-world title holder Trina Gulliver has also made her voice heard but until now no one really seems to be paying any attention.

However, at the 2012 Lakeside World Professional Darts Championships the girls took matters into their own hands deciding to fight for more women's darts on television and for more direct involvement in and control of their own futures.

Julie Lambie, secretary and player for Lincolnshire County darts, working with Sussex County player Luci Cunningham, organised an online petition regarding the lack of TV coverage for the ladies' game. This was supported at Lakeside by a number of top lady players including Deta Hedman. As a direct result of the petition, cable network ESPN agreed to allow the Lakeside Women's World Professional Darts Championship final to be shown on the red button.

THE LADIES DARTS ORGANISATION (LDO)

Spurred on by the success of the petition, a team of ladies led by Julie continued to champion their cause by creating an association totally devoted to the ladies' game; the Ladies Darts Organisation (LDO). Star players like Deta Hedman, Lorraine Farlam, Rhian Edwards and Linda Jones came on board with more 'names' joining on a regular basis. In addition, the LDO teamed up with the England Darts Organisation (EDO) to help promote the ladies' presence in the England Grosvenor Grand Prix of Darts and to assist in enhancing their overall presence in the sport.

A website —www.ladiesdartsorganisation.com — was set up, plus a Facebook group called 'Ladies Darts'. Already the LDO has made great strides in promoting the ladies' game so there seems little chance that this organisation will fail like the ill-fated Ladies Darts Association did a few years back. The first LDO Ladies Classic was held in 2012 at Rileys, Crofton Road, Lincoln, with Kent's Donna Rainsley beating Cheshire's Lorraine Farlam 7–6 in the final.

NOTABLE LADY DARTERS

Trina Gulliver

Surely top of anyone's list of female darts players must be the multi-world titled Trina Gulliver who won in 2001–2007, 2010 and 2011. 2012 was the first year that Trina did not make it to the women's Lakeside final. Part of the reason for that may well have been the death of her beloved mother Muriel only days before the tournament.

In 2012 Trina earned her 50th international cap and has captained England ladies to victory in both the singles and the pairs in the 1999, 2003, 2005 and 2011 WDF World Cups. She has also won the Winmau World Masters on a record-breaking five occasions.

At the time of writing Trina is in search of her 10th world title.

Deta Hedman

In 1997 Deta Hedman quit darts when she was at the top of her game having won numerous titles and collected her 19th consecutive 'Lady of the Match' award for Essex County. Olly Croft of the BDO called Deta's retirement 'one of the biggest disappointments of recent times'. Deta had become disillusioned with the game and the prize money on offer. In March 1997 she had topped the ladies' money list with £6,410; the previous year she had earned only £3,775!

Deta returned to darts in 2002 with the PDC and then retired again in the mid-2000s. Back with the BDO in 2010 Deta qualified for the Lakeside Women's World Championship but failed to make the final. In 2012 she made it to the final and at one stage led Russia's Anastasia Dobromyslova only to then lose 2–1.

Anastasia Dobromyslova

Russian-born Anastasia first came to the notice of the darts world when she won the 2001 Winmau Girls World Masters, beating Denmark's Jeanet Thomassen 3–1 in the final. Anastasia had been runner-up in the same event twelve months earlier.

In 2008 Anastasia became the first Russian darts player to win the Lakeside Women's World Professional Darts Championship, beating Trina Gulliver 2–0 and bringing the Golden Girl's run of seven consecutive titles to an end.

After winning the title Anastasia 'defected' to the PDC but returned to the BDO code in 2010. In 2012 Anastasia won her second world professional title against a resurgent Deta Hedman.

Lilian Barnett

History was made at the Rainbow Suite, Kensington, London, in 1985 when New Zealand darts player Lilian Barnett became the first non-British player to win the Winmau World Masters Ladies' Singles Championship. Lilian beat the 1983 Winmau champion, England's Sonya Ralphs, 3–1 in the final. Lilian told *Darts World* magazine, 'I only play darts once or twice a month; just when I feel like it.'

In 1989 Lilian had to give up darts due to a work-related injury but returned to the sport in 1994 where she continued to give both top New Zealand and Australian players a run for their money.

LADIES' SNIPPETS

LINDA RAISES THE BAR FOR CHARITY

Back in April 1986, when she was England's no. 1 lady darter, Linda Batten set the bar for other ladies when she hit a 117-dart 3,001 at her local pub, the Old Wheatsheaf in Enfield. Linda was being paced by future World Professional Darts Champion, Bob Anderson, who went out in 87 darts; she was a mere dozen darts short of the then existing men's record held by Mike Gregory. The match enabled Linda to raise over £1,500 for Arthritis Care.

A DROUGHT OF 180s

When the Ilford Borough Darts League (Ladies Section) was established in 1957 women signed up from all over the area, enjoying their matches and the opportunity to chat about everything and nothing. One subject that never came up until mid-1977 was the scoring of 180s. For nearly two decades no one in the league hit a maximum. Then on one single evening three players, Ivy Shoesmith, Mariene Britton and Norma O'Donoghue all hit 180s.

JUST WHAT THE DOCTORS ORDERED

In 1971 the ladies' darts team at the Royal Oak pub in Shaw, near Oldham, celebrated winning the Shaw Ladies' Friendly Darts League title with champagne provided by three doctors who regularly held meetings at the pub. The doctors had promised the ladies the booze if they could win the title at the first attempt, which they did.

Ladies' captain Dora Horton told the *Daily Mail*, 'They really kidded us when we started seven months ago. I think we deserve the champagne. We have worked really hard.'

THE PRETTY CHUCKER

That's the nickname given to Christine Ferris from Buckinghamshire back in the late 1960s. Within a fortnight of her boyfriend Marcus showing her how to play darts, Christine had taken his place in their local darts team at the Harrow pub. Christine, became a renowned darts ace over a period of a few months, beating 150 men to win the local darts league cup.

Christine told the *Daily Sketch*, 'One chap did not bow out of the cup competition all that gracefully. He picked his darts up and threw them on the floor. I cannot understand anyone getting upset by the game.'

DARTUS INTERRUPTUS

Up until November 1978 nothing, but nothing, prevented the ladies of the Wellington pub Haverton Hill, Middlesbrough, or the Astronaut, Billingham, from enjoying their darts.

But on that fateful evening when the teams were playing against each other in a friendly match, an empty runaway gas tanker crashed through a side wall of the darts room and reduced the place to rubble. Other regulars managed to free some of the women who had become trapped under the fallen masonry. Fortunately no one was seriously injured.

AND, REALLY, FINALLY . . .

One evening during the mid-1990s at a pub in Essex a lady darts player collapsed on the oche.

She was playing for a local Ladies' Licensed Victuallers' Association team in a vital league match. Her game was the last of the night but there was no undue pressure on her as her team had already secured victory. Witnesses stated that the lady toed the line, eyed the dartboard, went to throw, paused, held her head and collapsed on the oche. She was declared dead at the scene by the ambulance crew.

The landlady of the pub subsequently told a local journalist, 'She passionately loved darts.'

THAT'S A STRANGE LENGTH

Why on earth is the standard length of the oche (or 'throw-line', 'throw-off line' or 'hockey') used in almost every darts tournament around the globe 7ft 9¼in? That surely is a strange length.

When darts was originally standardised in the 1920s by the National Darts Association (NDA) the throw-line (or 'hockey' as it was called and spelt back then) was set at 9ft from a plumb line dropped from the face of the dartboard and then measured along the floor. Before that the lengths of oche varied from place to place, some being set as close as 6ft, while others were massively long – up to 10ft.

THE FIRST STANDARD HOCKEY

In 1927 when the NDA was called upon to organise the News of the World Individual Darts Championship, their 9ft throw was adopted. However, when the News of the World resumed after the Second World War in 1947/48, the throw-line was reduced to 8ft and this remained the standard in that and hundreds of other tournaments and leagues for many decades.

THE NDAGB LENGTH

In the early 1950s, when the National Darts Association of Great Britain (NDAGB) (which was nothing to do with the NDA) was formed, that organisation's rules included an oche length of 7ft 6in. This was to remain constant in all of the NDAGB tournaments until it was overwhelmed by the BDO in the mid-1970s.

THE BDO/WDF LENGTH

The BDO adopted the NDAGB oche length but after the World Darts Federation (WDF) was set up in 1977 its member countries looked for a 'world' standard length of throw, a happy medium between the NDAGB length and that of the News of the World of, say, 7ft 9in but instead of setting the standard at that, the WDF came up with 7ft 9¼in.

But why?

For many years it was believed and blogged that 7ft 9in did not 'translate' into metric (which was all the rage back in '77) but 7ft 9¼in did (2.37m) so that explained the strange length of oche. This author included this 'fact' in a Unicorn blog believing it to be true but then some wise person responded pointing out that 7ft 9¼in did *not* 'translate' into metric to 2.37m but 2.368852m.

On putting this to the WDF the truth was finally revealed. The measurement was never intended to be an 'exact' equivalent in metres but a compromise. At the WDF meeting at Wembley in 1977 where the very first WDF World Cup was discussed, the distance of 2.37m was adopted as the official WDF standard. It was proposed (it is believed by the Swedish delegate) that the 7ft 9¼in be adopted in its metric equivalent which happened to be extremely close to 2.37 metres. This was seconded and approved unanimously by all countries present.

The WDF members appreciated that this was not an exact conversion but decided to accept 2.37m as a compromise. After all, one could hardly expect tournament organisers to measure out a 2.368852m oche! (By the way, for those who appreciate such comparisons, the difference between 2.37m and 7ft 9¼in is almost exactly the thickness of a sheet of standard A4 printer paper.)

Months after the WDF meeting in 1977 the 7ft 9¼in throw-line was adopted as world standard for all major darts tournaments and this continues to be the case today.

BUT HANG ON . . .

Strangely enough, less than a year after the WDF decision, in 1978 at the inaugural Embassy World Professional Darts Championship the oche line was set at 7ft 6in, the same as that established by the NDAGB.

Stranger still, when the News of the World Individual Darts tournament was reintroduced for one year only in 1997 the throw-line was set, according to the rules in the tournament programme, at 7ft 9in; this despite the official world standard oche length being fixed at 7ft 9¼in by the World Darts Federation (WDF) two decades earlier. It was also a measurement never before used in the history of the News of the World competition.

AND WHY IS THE DARTBOARD SET UP 5ft 8in?

While the hockey/oche lengths have changed over the years the height of the dartboard from a plumb line from the centre of the bullseye to the floor has remained constant at 5ft 8in.

When the first rules of organised darts were introduced by the NDA in the mid-1920s it was specified that 'the board be 5ft 8in high from the floor to the centre [of the board]'.

This measurement was representative of the standard height of a man at that time.

DARTS MYTHOLOGY

THE 'LONDON' DARTBOARD IS THE SAME AS A 'CLOCK' BOARD

For more years than anyone in darts cares to remember it has been the common practice of darts writers to refer to the twenty-segmented dartboard used in all major competitions as either the 'London', 'Standard', 'Trebles' or 'Clock' board.

'London' is understandable as that was where the trebles and outer bull were added in the early twentieth century and the capital was the place where, in the 1920s, the first national darts association, cunningly named the National Darts Association (NDA), was founded.

'Standard' is self-explanatory as, especially since the 1970s, the board has become standard across the globe.

'Trebles' is OK too as this defines the difference between the Yorkshire Board, from which the standard board was born, the Yorkshire Board having no treble ring or outer bull.

However, the problem occurs with the 'Clock'. It simply does not make sense for a dartboard with twenty numbered segments to be described as a 'Clock' board as, and this is not news to anyone, a normal clock has, if it was divided up, twelve segments.

For years darts professional Bobby George has argued that the word 'Clock' refers to the East End 'Fives' dartboard which actually does have twelve numbered segments (5, 10, 15, 20, three times). Bobby insisted, 'The guys who set up the NDA back in 1925 got it wrong. They put it in their rule book and changed the face of darts history. That was that. No comeback.'

Now having researched further with his good friend Harry Kicks, Bobby has sorted the matter once and for all. Harry told Bobby that during the 1920s and '30s Jack Hood, a top dartboard manufacturer in the East End of London, made double-faced elm dartboards with the 'London' board on one side and the Fives 'Clock' board on the other.

According to Harry, Hood advertised these boards with the legend 'London/Clock Board' and it was this description that led to the belief that it was a one-sided 'London Clock Board'.

ROYAL APPROVAL – PLAYING AND WATCHING AND NOT

In January 2012 Zara Phillips and her husband Mike Tindall were spotted in the VIP area of the Ladbrokes.com World Darts Championship at Alexandra Palace.

Mike Tindall wore a pinstriped hat, over-sized glasses and a comedy beard, following very much in the tradition of such occasions; the wearing of fancy dress. The press loved it and Zara by all accounts was enjoying herself too.

But this was not the first occasion that a royal had attended a top darts tournament. Prince Harry attended the same event in 2011. The prince's penchant for the arrows had been revealed four years earlier when his father Prince Charles revealed that Harry was a great deal better than he was at darts.

But it is not just recently that members of the royal family have demonstrated an enthusiasm for darts. Some have simply watched while others have actually played. One in particular even mentioned darts in jest.

Here are some examples of royal personages who have either watched, enthused about or even played darts.

JUST WATCHING

HM The Queen

In December 2007 at the BBC Sports Personality of the Year awards Her Majesty the Queen's granddaughter, Zara Phillips revealed to Phil 'The Power' Taylor the little known fact that HM the Queen followed televised darts championships.

The *Sun* dubbed Her Majesty 'Liz "The Real Power" Windsor' and commented, 'Not since King Harold came a cropper at Hastings in 1066 has a British monarch been said to have had an eye for the arrers.'

Princess Anne

A fascinating royal dart fact was revealed by HRH Princess Anne in early 1984 during a BBC Radio Two interview with Gerald Williams. The princess told Williams that she and her husband Mark Phillips watched pretty much every televised sport including darts. Her Royal Highness added that she appreciated the skill factor involved at darts at the highest level.

WOW! What a recommendation!

As soon as the news reached the headquarters of the British Darts Organisation, top BDO man Olly Croft wrote a letter to Buckingham Palace inviting Princess Anne to grace a forthcoming tournament with her presence. Olly told reporters, 'It's an honour and a terrific boost to learn that darts has royal followers.'

The darts press and sympathetic national dailies were all over the story, while more cynical journalists saw the BDO being too presumptuous. One broadsheet journalist in particular, who admitted to his own 'morbid fascination with big-time darts', wrote that the BDO had invited the princess along 'to give her the privilege of seeing Eric, Jocky and the lads in the flesh, as it were.'

The BDO invitation was graciously declined.

Eric Bristow mentioned the royal watcher during an interview for the *Independent* in January 1989. He said, 'A lot of the royals watch darts. Princess Anne watches a lot of it on telly. It gives the game some pull in America and Canada.'

ROYAL PLAYERS

HRH Prince Charles

In February 2007 Prince Charles was spotted playing darts at a pub in Cumbria. One Sunday broadsheet reported that it was 'A terrible shame,' adding, 'apparently his mother had such high hopes for him.'

Undeterred by such comments, in March that same year the heir apparent spoke at Clarence House on the fifth anniversary of the establishment of his campaign to preserve rural pubs, 'Pub is the hub'. Prince Charles told those present, 'Whatever a gastro pub is, it seems to be threatening the future of pub darts which is rather worrying. My youngest son is a great deal better than I am [at darts] and you can guess why, but I am doing my best to keep the darts tradition going.'

Good for you, sir. Charlie really was becoming the darters' darling.

Prince William

An announcement on Prince Charles' website www.princeofwales.co.uk dated 7 December 2006 stated that 'Prince William visits the ICAP trading floor in London for the annual Global Charity Day'; ICAP being a voice and electronic dealer broker and provider of post-trade risk services.

This was a day when brokers dressed up in fancy dress costumes and where, more importantly, all revenue and commission from the day's trading went to charity. The Tusk Trust, of which Prince William is a patron, was one of the charities benefiting that year.

The image that accompanied the piece showed Prince William trying his hand at darts with ICAP brokers looking on.

Duke of Kent

In November 1976 the Duke of Kent visited the South London premises of darts giant Unicorn Products Ltd. The company had been singled out as a success story at the special export-drive conference at Croydon for their export performance and the Duke of Kent paid Unicorn a visit in his capacity as vice-president of the British Overseas Board of Trade. A photograph featured in *Darts World* magazine (December 1976) showed the duke trying his aim with the company's latest darts under the guidance of Barry Twomlow, at that time Unicorn's global darts ambassador.

Years earlier, in 1938, the charity the £oyal Society of Dartsmen (£.s.d., this acronym also referring to the currency at the time) was formed to raise money through darts for the voluntary hospitals. On 14 July that same year the then Duke of Kent 'kindly consented' to become the 100,000th member of the £.s.d.

During a special fundraising evening held at the Gaiety Theatre, London, on 6 December 1938 HRH the Duke of Kent KG, accepted an iron lung, together with a cheque for 1,000 guineas, on behalf of the British Charities Association. All the money had been raised by the £.s.d. This was long before the advent of the National Health Service and a time when hospitals' only funds were from charitable causes and generous benefactors.

Controversial if introduced today but not back then, the motto of the £.s.d. was 'Alms for the love of Arrers'.

PLAYING AND WATCHING

Queen Elizabeth the Queen Mother (God bless 'er)

On 17 December 1937 King George VI and Queen Elizabeth visited the Slough Social Centre and, while there, played a game of darts.

The king and queen were invited guests at the new centre and undertook an extensive tour of the building which included the games room where billiards, table tennis and darts were being played. Having watched a darts match in progress, unexpectedly, the queen asked one of the dart-players if she could try the game. After brief instructions on how to play, the royal match began. However, it was not a game of 301 or 501.

The queen threw first, scoring a single seven, a single thirteen and a single one, a total of 21 points. The king then took the darts and scored 19 points; the king then declared that the queen had won the match by 2 points. The Queen told darts players standing nearby that she thought it was 'a very sporty game'.

This brief involvement of the royal couple with darts was reported in the national daily newspapers, reference being made to a 'Royal Visit to Workers' Club' and 'The King and Queen Play "Darts"'.

The editor of Darts and Sports Weekly News on 25 December predicted that, by throwing only three darts, the queen would encourage thousands more women to follow her example and begin playing 'the world's most

fascinating game.' He was right as Mr R.B. Tillcock, Honorary Secretary of the British Darts Council (BDC), reported shortly afterwards that his organisation had been 'snowed under with inquiries' from thousands of women asking where they could obtain tuition in dart-throwing.

At Christmas 1992 on the popular TV series *Have I Got News for You*, quizmaster Angus Deaton commented, 'William Hill are offering 33-1 on *Eldorado* topping the TV ratings next year and 5-2 on Charles and Diana having another child.' He then added, 'I wonder what the odds are on the Queen Mother winning the Embassy Darts Classic'. Panellist Paul Merton immediately responded, 'She's been putting a lot of practice in. She's keen to get the title back.'

ANOTHER 'ROYAL' PLAYING

The Shah of Persia

Not one of 'our' royals but, back then, still a royal personage, the Shah of Persia and Queen Farah surprised Sunday lunchtime regulars at the Queen's Head pub at Newton, Cambridgeshire, in March 1965 by popping in for halves of bitter and a game of darts. Landlord Clifford Short said, 'We had heard that they might call in, but we didn't think they would have the time. Everyone carried on drinking and watching them play darts.'

The shah and Queen Farah had been staying at Newton Hall, only 300 yards away, the home of Lord Walston who, at the time, was Parliamentary Under-Secretary of State at the Foreign Office. They were in the UK on an unofficial visit.

NOT WATCHING OR PLAYING

Sarah Ferguson

Not recorded as ever toeing the oche, Fergie is reported as making reference to our sport in 1992 when visiting a centre for brain-injured children. After having a photograph taken with one brave youngster Fergie turned to the child and said, 'Well done . . . You can take the photo home and throw darts at it.'

LET'S TALK DARTS

Nowadays when you think of darts language it tends to be restricted to what viewers hear on TV such as the ribald remarks of the commentators and the 'One hunnnnnndrrrred and eiiiiiiiiiiiightyyyyyyy' and 'Yeeeeeeeesssss, that's game-shot and the match to . . .' from the enthusiastic referee or assorted advice and encouragement shouted by the audience when they believe that their favourite player is underperforming. But in the past the oches of Britain were alive to all sorts of expressions that meant something to the players and watchers but probably nothing to those 'outside' of darts.

LANGUAGE OR LINGO?

Richard Holt in his classic sports history work *Sport and the British – A Modern History* (1989) wrote that 'Darts is a good example of the power of popular culture to create private languages for players,' while John Moore, in his book, *Brensham Village* (1946) really hit the nail on the head when he wrote, 'darts has its own esoteric terminology, some of which is common to the whole country and some of which is probably local. It is a language of association, with a bit of rhyming slang mixed up in it.'

Bobby George was even more succinct in his book *Scoring for Show, Doubles for Dough – Bobby George's Darts Lingo* (2011) when he wrote, 'Part of the fun is when players use certain words to brighten up a game. (And by that I don't mean "F*** off! I'm trying to concentrate!")'

FAMILIAR

Here is just a small selection of expressions that are so ingrained into the English language that, even today, they can be heard on most casual oches.

Bed and Breakfast

A score of 26 with three darts, usually single five, single twenty, single one. The expression derives from 2s 6d (spoken as 'two and six'), in the old British currency; the amount being the cost of bed and breakfast in modest hostelries in the 1920s when modern darts was still in its infancy.

Clickety-click

66. One of many darts expressions derived from the game of bingo which, believe it or not, started out as a darts game in English fairgrounds.

Madhouse

An expression meaning that the player has ended up on double one. Just like being sent to the madhouse, the player has nowhere else to go.

Mugs away

The person who lost the previous game is allowed to start first in the next. The reference to 'mugs' means that the loser buys the winner a mug of beer and not that he or she is a mug.

Shanghai

The word 'shanghai' comes from nautical slang and means 'to drug or otherwise render insensible, and ship on board a vessel wanting hands.' Nowadays, in a general sense 'shanghai'ed' means anything that has interrupted someone's actions or train of thought, for example, 'The boss then shanghai'ed the meeting and talked about nothing but himself for the rest of the morning.'

In the darts sense it means that, by hitting single, double and treble with one turn of three darts, you have effectively 'shanghai'ed' the rest of the players out of the game – something none of them wanted to happen.

Top of the shop

This refers to the double right at the top of the standard dartboard, double twenty. The opposite, 'Bottom of the shop' is rarely, if ever, used but if it is then it will refer to double three.

LOCAL

These few examples are specific to a single area.

Lord Sherborne

One of the oldest 'local' darts expressions from Gloucestershire in about 1935, used to represent the number 33. Lord Sherborne, who resided at that time at Sherborne Park near Northleach, owned a car – an uncommon sight in those days – which bore the number 33.

Lumbs

In the 1980s this word 'used back in the old days' in Hornsey, north London, was called when a player required eleven or double eleven to finish; the reason being that Lumbs' was a well-established pawnbroker known by everyone in the area based at 11 High Street.

Style and Winch

A Kent darting expression from the late 1930s/early 1940s meaning 26. Style and Winch were a Kentish brewery but why it should be linked to the number 26 is not known.

MORE RECENT DISCOVERIES

What follows are a number of relatively new darts expressions never published in book form before, collected and contributed by Lee Bennett of www.dartsmad.com.

All the gear, no idea

You know the kind of person; they turn up with the latest super-duper titanium tungsten signature darts that have cost them a small fortune. The darts are housed in a nice shiny case chock full of quality top-of-the-range spare flights plus darts sharpener.

The player then proceeds to demonstrate that he/she couldn't hit a barn door and don't even make it on to the reserve list of their local pub team.

Byooooworr!

This expression is a conjoining of two statements from the north of England meaning a nearly-but-not-quite-great shot.

The player has 100 left. He hits single twenty and then decides to finish with a flourish and go for two double tops; a risky outshot. He then hits the first double top and the second looks like it has gone in but is slightly obscured. It isn't in. It's bent the wire.

From the onlookers the player hears one begin to shout 'Beautiful darts' before they realise the third dart has not found its target. 'Beautiful darts' turns into 'awww unlucky' half way through and ends up as 'byooooworr'.

Couldn't hit a cow's arse with a banjo

An expression used to describe someone who is not very good at darts.

Flukey Treb/Flukey Dub

When playing the alternative darts game of Tactics 'up north' you have to knock off three doubles and three trebles as well as the numbers and the bull.

Landing a fortunate dart in a treble or double that you were not aiming for will draw a groan from your opponent and is known as a 'flukey treb' or 'flukey dub'. Once you have hit three, it's 'trebs off' or 'dubs off'.

These flukes can often be the difference between winning and losing in Tactics.

One in the Ax

This is a statement made when a dart falls from the board on to the floor. Axminster is of course a renowned manufacturer of quality carpets. The fact that darters are hardly likely to find themselves walking up and down an oche made of finest Axminster gives this phrase its comedy element.

The expression is also a distant cousin to the much older 'Sloppy sailor' which refers to a bounce-out – 'A sloppy sailor; always on the deck'.

Shit! Cack! Redeemer!

These words follow each score in a three-dart combination that starts off badly but then improves. For example, the first dart hits a single one ('shit!'), the second throw is a dart in single five ('cack!') but then the third dart hits the treble twenty ('redeemer!').

Top Bollocks

One of many expressions for double top, this one being derived from the northern England saying 'She's got a great pair of top bollocks' which is used when referring to a well-endowed female.

In modern times there have not been so many new words and phrases introduced into darts lingo. Perhaps the most recent has been the persistence of darts commentators to refer to the treble twenty segment as 'the lipstick' in preference to the previously popular 'red bit'.

For personalised darts language you could do no better than learn from the master and go to www.sidwaddell.com.

DARTS MYTHOLOGY

DARTS WAS TAKEN TO AMERICA ON THE MAYFLOWER IN 1620

The 'fact' that darts was exported to America on board the *Mayflower* in 1620 is probably *the* most repeated piece of darts history you will ever read or hear.

THE MYTH

It is so simple and so succinct. Just imagine the scenario. English folk who love playing darts were persecuted for their religious beliefs, flee the country by boat to find a new life in the New World and, quite naturally of course, take England's most popular pub recreation with them on board, namely darts.

For a long time this 'fact' has been accepted as legitimate darts history, so much so that it appears regularly in pub quizzes.

Question:	What English game was taken to America on *The Mayflower* in 1620?
Answer:	Darts.
Real answer?	Well, it was definitely *not* darts.

The passengers on board the *Mayflower* were Puritans who detested everything and anything to do with alcohol and the alehouse. Thus there was no way they would ever promote such an activity. Their religious doctrine simply did not allow it – darts was contrary to everything they stood for.

Imagine the captain of the *Mayflower* locking up his house as he prepared to leave England for the last time, then, tapping his top pocket, pausing and turning to his betrothed and saying, 'Forsooth my love. I have lefteth my darts in myst bedside table. Please goeth and retrieveth them for me.'

THOSE RESPONSIBLE

A darts book published in the late 1960s started it all. The author wrote, 'It has been said that the Pilgrim Fathers amused themselves by playing darts aboard the *Mayflower* in the year 1620.' By the late 1970s, the myth was appearing in darts books whenever the history of the sport was mentioned. One volume published in America recalled 'there are references, in the *Mayflower's* logs, to darts as a pastime of the Pilgrims on board the vessel.'

At about the same time, over in the UK, another author declared that 'Crude "darts" are said to have been used by the Pilgrim Fathers on board the *Mayflower* as they sailed to the New World in 1620.' But the seal of approval to this dollop of fiction came in 1973 when an entry in the *Encyclopaedia Britannica* (14th edition) read 'Darts is recorded as a pastime of the Pilgrim Fathers on board the Mayflower in 1620.'

It must be true then. (Not!)

THE TRUTH

This myth was finally dispelled by research published in 2001 by American darts researcher, historian and fellow mythbuster, Dan William Peek in his book *To the Point – The Story of Darts in America*. Dan discovered that there is no mention of darts in the log of the *Mayflower* and no evidence whatsoever that darts arrived in the USA by that route.

Recent evidence suggests that Irish immigrants took the game to America in the late Victorian/early Edwardian period. At that time, it had limited impact, remaining more a child's toy than an adult recreation for many decades. Previous to that the Native Americans had been making makeshift darts for centuries from such things as corn cobs.

Darts became increasingly popular in the USA and Canada after the Second World War when military personnel stationed in Britain visited the traditional English pubs, became fascinated by darts and eventually took the game home with them.

Today, depending on where you live in North America, electronic, soft-tip darts vies for popularity with the traditional steel-tip game. Companies from within the USA and Europe have tried to sell back darts to the UK in the electronic form but so far all attempts have failed miserably. UK darters (a) don't appreciate their game being messed about with and (b) will never pay to play.

PHIL TAYLOR'S BIG SIXTEEN

Between November 1996 and March 2012 Phil 'The Power' Taylor had scored no less than sixteen perfect nine-dart games of 501 in major tournaments. He has, of course, scored many more in practice. Nearly six years elapsed between his first and second nine-darters in top competition but after that they came thick and fast.

At the time of writing Phil Taylor is top in the nine-darter charts with Dutch star Raymond van Barneveld biting at his heels and England's James Wade and Australia's Simon Whitlock in joint third place with four apiece.

Even though Barney is not that far away, one thing is certain – 'The Power' will always be looking to stay in front. So, as the man who sets the bar for all other darts players in all aspects of the sport, it is singularly appropriate that Phil's 'big sixteen' nine-darters are recorded here.

Date:	17 November 1996
Tournament:	Primus Belgian Masters
Venue:	Houthalen, Belgium
Opponent:	Dennis Priestley (England)
Round:	Final

Date:	1 August 2002
Tournament:	World Matchplay
Venue:	Blackpool, UK
Opponent:	Chris Mason (England)
Round:	Quarter-final

Date:	5 June 2004
Tournament:	UK Open Finals
Venue:	Bolton, UK
Opponent:	Matt Chapman (England)
Round:	Last 32

Date:	12 June 2005
Tournament:	UK Open Finals
Venue:	Bolton, UK
Opponent:	Roland Scholten (Netherlands)
Round:	Semi-final

Date:	8 May 2007
Tournament:	International Darts League
Venue:	Nijmegen, Netherlands
Opponent:	Raymond van Barneveld
Round:	2nd Phase Group, 1st round of matches

Date:	9 June 2007
Tournament:	UK Open Finals
Venue:	Bolton, UK
Opponent:	Wes Newton
Round:	Last 32

Date:	23 March 2008
Tournament:	Players' Championship
Venue:	Bad Soden, Germany
Opponent:	Ronnie Baxter (England)
Round:	Last 16

Date:	7 June 2008
Tournament:	UK Open Finals
Venue:	Bolton, UK
Opponent:	Jamie Harvey (Scotland)
Round:	Last 32

Date:	15 September 2009
Tournament:	Championship League
Venue:	Crondon Park, UK
Opponent:	John Part (Canada)
Round:	Group 1, 4th round of matches

Date:	24 May 2010 (1)
Tournament:	Premier League
Venue:	Wembley, UK
Opponent:	James Wade (England)
Round:	Final

Date:	24 May 2010 (2)
Tournament:	Premier League
Venue:	Wembley, UK
Opponent:	James Wade (England)
Round:	Final

Date:	2 October 2011
Tournament:	Players' Championship
Venue:	Dublin, Republic of Ireland
Opponent:	Kevin McDine
Round:	Last 64

Date:	20 October 2011
Tournament:	Championship League
Venue:	Crondon Park, UK
Opponent:	Mervyn King
Round:	Final Group, 3rd round of matches

Date:	16 February 2012
Tournament:	Premier League
Venue:	Aberdeen, UK
Opponent:	Kevin Painter (England)
Round:	Week 2

Date:	10 March 2012
Tournament:	Players' Championship
Venue:	Reading, UK
Opponent:	Peter Hudson (England)
Round:	Last 128

Date:	11 March 2012
Tournament:	Players' Championship
Venue:	Reading, UK
Opponent:	Tony West (England)
Round:	Last 64

Perhaps the most fascinating fact in relation to these sixteen nine-darters is that on every occasion when Phil hit a perfect game, he also went on the win the tournament.

WALK-ON GIRLS

The glamorous walk-on girls are now a popular feature and fixture of every major Professional Darts Corporation tournament, leading the gladiatorial darters through the throng of banner-waving fans accompanied by the darts players' walk-on music. The girls arrive on stage and pose as each darts player shakes hands with the officials and his opponent. The girls then walk off to wolf-whistles and shouts of joy from the overheated male members of the crowd while on stage, battle commences.

THE FIRST WALK-ON GIRLS

The BDO were the first to introduce walk-on girls at major tournaments and presentations back in 1977. The event was the World Cup and the venue the Wembley Conference Centre. Olly Croft's daughters Elaine and Lesley, dressed in long white dresses and wearing sashes, led the players on to the stage. The Croft girls were also featured at that year's Winmau World Masters but then the BDO changed tack.

Instead of walk-on girls a recorded fanfare accompanied the players as they walked to the stage and later still a BDO official carrying the appropriate country's flag would lead the individual players on to the oche. However, the latter, according to Olly Croft was mainly for 'security purposes'.

But it was the PDC and Sky that reintroduced the walk-on girls in the late 1990s.

THE GIRLS

The 2012 Ladbrokes.com World Championships featured models Kelly Donegan, Nicola Cowell, Hazel O'Sullivan and Sarah Tunnicliffe. Those four girls were featured in the 2012 McCoy's Premier League Darts plus Jacqui Adams, Erica Wild and Holly Johnson although for the Scottish leg local models were featured.

Models Karen Smith and Sue Willets were the first PDC walk-on girls, appearing at the inaugural World Matchplay in 1994. The venue was the Winter Gardens, Blackpool, and the tournament was sponsored by Proton Cars. First to be led on stage by Karen and Sue were Eric Bristow and Dennis Priestley. Karen and Sue featured in the walk-ons for Sky and the PDC for four years then set themselves up in business in 1998, a model agency called Angels Elite Models, and they have continued to supply the walk-on girls to the PDC ever since.

You might have thought that in 1994 the introduction of walk-on girls to top-flight darts and amazing darts being played throughout the tournament would have been enough excitement for one tournament, but no. Another surprise was in store for the fans at the Winter Gardens as they watched, stunned, as US star darter Larry Butler from Dayton, Ohio, wrested the title from the grasp of England's Dennis Priestley by a margin of 16–12 in a nailbiting finale.

A QUESTION OF BALANCE

In 2009 top lady darter Anastasia Dobromyslova qualified for the Ladbrokes.com PDC World Darts Championship held at the Alexandra Palace, London. Clearly it would have been inappropriate to have a walk-on girl accompany her to the stage so for balance the PDC provided a 'walk-on man'. Anastasia lost 6–3 in the Preliminary Round to Dutch qualifier Remco van Eilden.

THE GIRLS WHO WALKED ON AND PLAYED DARTS

Way back in the late 1970s as darts was emerging as a serious spectator sport, and before the politically correct brigade came along and spoiled things for everyone, there were the Halex Darts Dollies. The brainchild of Judy Sharp, Marketing Manager for Halex Sports, the company selling dartboards, darts, shafts and flights, the Dollies were a tremendous success live on stage at a time when darts was still very much part of a man's world and the vast majority of spectators were men too.

'What better way,' said Judy, 'to attract the attention of darts players – potential customers for our products – than with some very attractive young ladies who also happened to be excellent darts players? Enter the Halex Darts Dollies. It was blatant sexist marketing – and it was very successful!'

The widely publicised search for Dollies ended at Butlins at Clacton-on-Sea, Essex, in early 1979. The original Dollies were Janis Gullaine, Chrissy Smith, Janette Sontag and Sharon Vandenburgh; all attractive ladies and all darts players. The Dolly 'uniform' comprised a silky green polo shirt and a very short dark green skirt (from the company's schools' sportswear range), frilly underwear, high-heeled silver strappy shoes and beauty queen style silky sashes.

The Dollies were an instant hit. They supported the Embassy exhibition tours around huge beery, smoky clubs and always received a rapturous reception. Punters were invited on stage to 'play with a Dolly'. Invariably, the Dolly would drop a dart and bend over to pick it up, always causing a cheer. If the Dolly won, the punter got a set of Dolly flights and a big 'Halex Darts Dollies played with me' badge. If he won, he received a top of the range set of Halex darts – and a kiss from the Dolly!

The Halex Darts Dollies toured all over the UK, with the Embassy tour and in their own right, raising money for charity along the way. Judy said, 'They were hugely popular and may well have contributed to introducing the game to more ladies who had previously been intimidated by its masculine image. The girls loved the spotlight and the attention, and being Dollies helped their careers enormously. It was blatantly sexist, yes, but it was also brilliant marketing: harmless fun, not degrading in any way, and it was absolutely right for the time.'

But would such an idea work today?

Call the Politically Correct Police!

DUTCH COURAGE AND DETERMINATION

When the list of competitors for the 2012 Lakeside World Professional Darts Championship was published in late 2011 it read more like a European international darts match than a world tournament. Take out the 23 players from the UK and you were left with nine; eight of which were Dutch, the other a Belgian.

SEALED WITH A KIST

Despite the lack of participants from other nations the Lakeside produced some amazing matches, especially in the final where the Dutch debutant and 66-1 outsider 25-year-old Christian Kist, ranked 106th in the world rankings up until that time, saw off the determined challenge of the no. 8 seed, Tony O'Shea 7–5.

Kist, a Dutch international and a road worker by trade, had qualified through the tough international play-offs and reached the last 16 of the prestigious Winmau World Masters at Hull in 2011. TV pundits dubbed him 'The Lipstick' (Kist – Lipstick, geddit?) during the early stages of the tournament and Bobby George noted Kist as a potential threat.

On his way to the title Kist defeated his fellow countryman, the no. 6 seed and 2011 semi-finalist Jan Dekker 3–2 in the first round, Belgian Geert de Vos 4–2 in round two, England's Alan Norris 5–1 in the quarter-finals and Ted Hankey (no. 15 seed) 6–5 in the semi-final.

This is not the first time that a Dutch debutant had triumphed at Lakeside. In 2006 21-year-old Jelle Klassen was crowned the youngest winner of the Lakeside as he defeated the four-time Lakeside World Champion, Dutch legend Raymond van Barneveld, 7–5 at Frimley Green.

BARNEY'S THE MAN

It was van Barneveld's initial world triumph in 1998 beating Wales' Richie Burnett (the 1995 Embassy World Champion) 6–5 that stimulated the craze for darts in The Netherlands. It gained a further boost in the following year when Barney retained his title with victory over England's Ronnie Baxter by a similar scoreline.

In 2003 Barney was again World Champion beating Wales' Ritchie Davies 6–3 in the final. His last Lakeside World Championship win was in 2005 when he beat England's Martin Adams 6–2. In 2006 Barney transferred his allegiance to the PDC. He had to wait less than a year to be crowned World Champion on his debut under the PDC code. In the 2007 final he beat Phil Taylor at the Circus Tavern, Purfleet, with a stunning comeback from three sets down to take the title 7–6 in the eleventh 'sudden death' leg.

THE FIRST FINALIST

To find the very first Dutch qualifier for what was then the Embassy World Professional Darts Championship you must travel back to 1988 when Bert Vlaadingerbroek played at the Lakeside Country Club. Unfortunately he was knocked out in the first round, going down to Northern Ireland's Fred McMullen 3–1. Bert was to return to Lakeside in 1989 (first round exit to England's Dennis Hickling 3–0), 1990 (first round exit 3–2 to eventual losing semi-finalist 'Big Cliff' Lazarenko) and 1992 another first round exit to Wales' Martin Phillips with a 3–0 scoreline.

ORIGINS

The actual origins of darts in The Netherlands can be traced back to the British Legion clubs set up in that country after the Second World War by ex-patriots who decided to settle in Holland.

This was the original stimulus for the game but it was Barney with his 1998 and 1999 World Championship wins who can be held totally responsible for generating the interest in competitive darts in his country which inevitably led to the rise of the 'Orange Army'.

For a short time during the late 1990s and early 2000s, darts was more popular in The Netherlands than football.

DARTS MYTHOLOGY

ANNE BOLEYN GAVE KING HENRY VIII A SET OF DARTS FOR HIS BIRTHDAY

Darts history was distorted again during the 1970s when a proven fact fell victim to journalistic licence.

THE NEARLY MYTH

In his 1973 autobiography *Darts*, dart player Tom Barrett declared 'Darts – or dartes as it was known in the days when Anne Boleyn gave a set to her beloved King Henry VIII – is one of our oldest and most popular sports.' Borrowing from that theme in 1977 an American darts writer declared with confidence, 'We know that Anne Boleyn gave her fickle king a set of jewel-encrusted darts for his birthday.' Thus presumably proving that during his turbulent reign and while perusing six wives and countless mistresses King Henry VIII found enough time to show an interest in the game of darts.

THE TRUTH

On the face of it, that sounds feasible. Indeed, a document registered in the Osterreichisches Staatsarchiv (the Austrian State Archive) in Vienna and dated 4 January 1532, written by the Austrian Emperor's Ambassador, Ernest Chapuys, verifies the presentation of Anne's gift to the king and his to her.

Written in French, when a section is translated it reveals that 'from her, he received special darts, richly ornamented in Biscayan fashion. And he in return, presented her with a room hung with tapestries . . .' The happy couple were exchanging New Year gifts, not celebrating King Henry's birthday.

Darts as we know the game today was not played in Tudor times. Research shows that the 'dartes' were eighteen-inch hand-held missive weapons used in hunting wild boar (hunting wild boar was probably King Henry's second most favourite passion).

A weapon known as a 'dart' or 'darte' existed in the sixteenth century and references to King Henry VIII playing darts have led to misinterpretation and the assumption that the pub game was thriving in the Tudor period. Alison Weir, writing about the King's penchant for wild boar hunting, refers to the New Year's gift in her book *Henry VIII and His Court* (2002) and states that the darts were 'probably hunting spears'.

FURTHER TUDOR DARTING

Other forms of darts were used in Tudor England. Darts, or more accurately 'darts for wildfire' were utilised to set fire to enemy sails and were normally thrown by hand. They appear in the inventory of 'The Sovereign', part of King Henry VIII's fleet. 'Dartes . . . lvij dossen' are listed immediately after the entry for 'Javelyns' in an inventory for the

Henry Grace a Dieu compiled in 1514. The *Mary Rose* inventory dated 1546 lists forty dozen 'dartes for tops', 'tops' being the fighting tops on the masts. These 'dartes for tops' were missive weapons, small spears or javelins, thrown from the fighting tops situated on the masts and were not dissimilar to 'darts for wildfire.' Most warships of the period were armed with darts; the *Mary Rose* by no means being unique in this respect.

'Dartes for tops' were thrown by hand and so there appears no reason why they could not be thrown for amusement too.

DARTS TUITION BY THE EXPERTS

Nowadays anyone interested in learning the finer points of darts play can visit any number of websites and receive tuition from well-known and many more not-really-very-well-known-at-all experts.

RUPERT CROFT-COOKE

The first 'expert' to teach people to play darts was itinerant author Rupert Croft-Cooke in 1936 in his book *Darts*. Croft-Cooke was an enthusiastic amateur player and hated formal rules for the game preferring to play to the 'house rules' wherever he went. However, he did reproduce the rules of the London Darts Club in his book for those more serious players 'who would like to have an applicable ruling on each point that may arise.' (He later admitted that the London Darts Club never existed except in his head and that he had made the rules up.)

Selected tip:
'[Darts] is a game to play with the golden glow of beer in one's brain, to the sound of tinkling glasses.'

A. WELLINGTON

In 1938, hot on the heels of the success of *Darts*, came the publication of *The Various Darts Games and How to Play Them* by A. Wellington, this book responding, like Croft-Cooke, to the increased interest of the middle and upper classes in the game of darts. Among the 'various darts games' were Shanghai, Round the Clock and Cricket.

Selected tip*:*
'It is . . . bad form to take a player's darts out of the board for him. You may damage his flights and some players are very touchy about their darts.'

JOHN YOUNG

John Young's *How to Play Darts & New Games for the Dart Board* was published in 1939. He wrote that darts was 'coming into its own' and was 'no longer looked down upon . . . by those who condemn anything associated with public houses.' Surprisingly when Young's book was relaunched 42 years later in 1981 and retitled *Winning Darts*, the text looked remarkably similar!

Selected tip *(1939):*
Lighting: 'When playing in the daylight, of course, it is best for the board to be fixed on the side of the room opposite to the window, so that players have their backs to the window when throwing.'

Selected tip *(1981):*
Lighting: 'When playing in the daylight, of course, it is best for the board to be fixed on the side of the room opposite to the window, so that players have their backs to the window when throwing.'

GEORGE CALEY

The first darts player to teach us to take darts tuition seriously was the East Anglian champion George Caley whose book *How to Improve Your Darts* appeared in 1950. Full of helpful advice and guidance (not to mention twenty-four 'action photos') Caley revealed his three 'Golden Rules' of play:

Golden Rule no. 1	A firm stance at the hockey
Golden Rule no. 2	The 'Double Pivot' Action of elbow and wrist
Golden Rule no. 3	The full Follow Through

These key rules have changed little over the intervening years merely being rephrased and embossed by those who followed.

Selected tip:
Stance: 'Adopt a natural, easy stance . . . stand rock-firm. Don't flex the knees. Don't move the head. Don't move the shoulders. Don't lean forward. Don't crane the neck. Don't sway from the hips. Don't stoop. Don't throw so that a jerk seems to run through your body. Don't rise on your heels.'

Even today some top darts players *still* do not heed this advice.

NOEL E. WILLIAMSON

It was to be nearly two decades before self-styled Hertfordshire player and darts coach Noel E. Williamson published his book *Darts* (there's that catchy title again!) in 1968.

Selected tip:
How to throw: 'Don't try to impersonate the statue of Eros, with one leg raised, that way you are off balance and lose your accuracy.'

GEORGE HAKIM

George Hakim, a player who confessed to 'eat, sleep and drink darts', wrote *The Darts Players' Handbook* published in 1977. His book was later to be revised and updated and included in the popular 'Teach Yourself' series.

Selected tip:
Form: 'Form is strange; it comes mysteriously, and its loss is only temporary in a player of proven ability. Its fluctuations should not upset him.'

As the 1970s progressed and the darts boom took hold and the first full-time darts professionals were established thus generating a demand for their presence and skills on the global oche, it was clearly time for the men who now earned their living from darts to reveal the secrets of their success. First off the mark was Leighton Rees.

LEIGHTON REES

Wales' Leighton Rees won the inaugural Embassy World Professional Darts Championship title in 1978 at the Heart of the Midlands Club, Nottingham. Already in demand as an exhibition player, a market for both his life story and his advice on how to play led to the publication of *Leighton Rees on Darts* in 1979. Part-tuition book and part-autobiography this was the first book written during the modern era of darts to reveal personal details of a player's life and times combined with the secrets of how to become a top player.

Selected tip:
Practice: 'Theories, formulae, observation, correct equipment, even a couple of pints – all of these are important factors in dartsplay. But far and away the most crucial ingredient in improving your play is *practice*. It is probably the only way too.'

JOHN LOWE

The following year, hard on Leighton's heels was the man Rees beat in the first Embassy in 1978 and the winner of the return match in the final of 1979, John Lowe.

Coincidentally titled *John Lowe On Darts* (1980) (and subtitled *Winning Darts the John Lowe Way*), in his book Lowe 'outlined the basics of darts' in a clear and concise way. Twenty-nine years later, in 2009, Lowe's advice was significantly updated in his second tuition book *The Art of Darts* which, for the first time in any book about the sport, featured a 'bonus masterclass' on how to become a professional darts player.

Never one to allow the grass to grow under his oche, in the summer of 1983 John Lowe became the first British darts player to produce a video cassette on how to play the game. Entitled *Darts – The John Lowe Way*, he demonstrated the skills of the sport and was interviewed by Phil Jones. The video also featured Surrey's Ritchie Gardner.

Selected tip *(1980):*
Safety: 'Never fix your board to a door that is used for access unless you can lock the door when playing. And never throw darts when there are small children around.'

Selected tip *(2009):*
Confidence: 'The most difficult thing when you play competitive darts at any level is mastering your mind. If you have a negative approach, for whatever reason, you will not play well. You must be in a positive frame of mind.'

DAVE WHITCOMBE

At one time among the youngest professional darts players on the TV darts circuit, England's Dave Whitcombe was an up-and-coming star of the sport and would go on to win the News of the World Individual Darts Championship title in 1989 and reach the Embassy World Professional Darts Championship finals on two occasions (1984 and 1986), losing in both to Eric Bristow.

While still on the way up Dave was called upon to write his own tuition book. Published in 1981 and including some brief autobiographical material, *How to Play Darts* comprised only 64 pages but, even so, included some great advice. Whitcombe was later to confess, 'That book took me about a fortnight to write – three weeks tops' which must be a record for any darts publication.

Selected tip:
Common courtesy: 'While your opponent is taking his shot, never rattle loose change in your pockets, deliberately fiddle with your darts, chink glasses or make any unnecessary sounds which might disturb him.'

Curiously, when Dave's book was first published, the front cover featured an image not of Dave but of Eric Bristow. This was, not surprisingly, changed for the reprint in 1988. This time John Lowe was on the cover!

ERIC BRISTOW

Some people must have wondered why it had taken 'The Crafty Cockney' so long to put pen to paper (ably assisted by his manager Dick Allix) and reveal his secrets of success. *Darts – A Complete Guide to the Game* was published in 1985, shortly after Bristow won his fourth Embassy title.

Anyone buying the book second-hand might be puzzled by the statement on page 33 that 'The set of darts with this pack are brass.' Uniquely *Darts – A Complete Guide to the Game* was sold only as part of a gift pack which included a set of 'Crafty Cockney' darts.

Selected tip:
Rhythm and throw: 'There should be no interruption of the flow of all three darts. It's a question of rhythm. If you hesitate, either from miscounting or looking for a number, then the all-important rhythm and flow may be gone. It all comes from practice.'

Eric's throw was later severely interrupted when he suffered for some time from dartitis.

CO STOMPE

One of the few non-English darts players to produce a darts tuition book is The Netherlands' Co Stompe. Quarter-finalist in both the PDC World Darts Championships of 2009 and 2010, Stompe's *Let's Play Darts* was published in 2007, not surprisingly, in Dutch.

Selected tip:
Trippels: 'Je kunt ere en spelelement in aanbrengen door met twee personen teglijk te trainen en tegen elkaar een wedstrijd te gooien wie het eerst tien trippels weet te raken van een bepaald getal.'

ELSEWHERE

Players and researchers in the USA continue to produce fascinating darts tuition books with titles including *Good Darts – Improving your game with psychological and self-mastery skills* (1994), which came with an accompanying cassette tape) by Gary R. Low PhD; Timothy R. Bucci's *A Quiver of 3 – Soft-tip darts for the new player* (2005); George Silberzahn's *How to Master the Sport of Darts* (Second edition, 2008) and Mike Orav's *Become Your Darts – An Enlightening Guide to Better Darting*.

So far the only woman to write a darts tuition book was USA darts enthusiast Madeline Dolowich whose *The Dart Book* was published in 1978.

Selected Dolowich tip:
Storage of darts: 'Never put your darts in the pocket of your pants or coat. Besides, if you sit down, you could have a nasty wound!'

DR DARTS

Back in the UK this author has also written a tuition book. Titled *The Official Bar Guide to Darts*, it was published in New York in 2010.

In 2011 darts professional Bobby George commented, 'This is The Professor's detailed guide to how to play and I have to say it ain't half bad bearing in mind that he's won f**k all decent darts competitions.'

Thanks Bobby.

So who's next?

Surely a certain Mr Taylor should have a go . . .

DARTEFACTS
ODDS AND OCHES

TOO DANGEROUS TO PLAY

When on a cycling tour in 1956 two men booked themselves into the YMCA at Achnashellach in the Scottish Highlands and then popped into a pub and ordered a couple of pints.

Espying a dartboard they asked the barman for a set of darts but he refused to give them to them. The time was 6.00 p.m. and the pub was empty. Asked why their request had been refused the barman explained, 'It's Saturday and you canny have darts on a Saturday in case somebody gets hurt.'

COULD WE START THE GAME NOW PLEASE?

Even in top darts tournaments who throws first in a match is determined by 'bulling up', that is, throwing for the bull's-eye, the nearest the centre starting the match. This method is also used to determine who will throw first in a deciding leg where the match is tied and it moves into a 'sudden death' situation. Many times have witnesses of televised darts seen this on their screens and fans are surprised if three or four darts have to be thrown to decide who throws first. This normally takes no more than two throws.

But what about taking fourteen darts?

In 1973 in the semi-final of the Branstone and Wolstone League (Warwickshire) pairs competition, representatives of the Glade team (Ken Gridle and Tony Wilcox) and the Union Jack (Trevor Peachey and Baz Ismay) were level at one game all in a best of three games match.

To decide who threw first in the deciding game, Ken and Baz threw for bull. Ken went first, his dart hitting the 25 (outer bull). Baz followed also scoring a 25. Baz then threw another 25 and Ken hit one too. Both then scored another 25. Baz's fifth and sixth darts were 25s and so were Baz's.

Finally, Ken just missed the 25 with his seventh dart, it landing outside the area of the outer bull while Baz made no mistake so at last the game could begin.

Baz and his partner Trevor Peachey (the 1956 News of the World Individual Darts Champion) went on to win the game.

THAT'S AN ODD THING TO DO

It is a little-known fact that Leighton Rees, the winner of the inaugural Embassy World Professional Darts Championship in 1978 threw darts of differing weights but not all three were different. Two were 27g followed by the third which weighed 31g.

His Welsh compatriot and great friend, the equally famous Alan Evans threw three different weights, 21, 21½ and 22g.

When Stan Outten, representing the Seven Kings Hotel, Ilford, defeated T. Hares of Ashford, Middlesex 2–1 to win the News of the World London and Home Counties Division championship in 1937, he did so with a 117 game-shot, using three odd brass darts.

STEP DOWN TO THE
OCHE PLEASE

When the popularity of darts surged in the 1920s and '30s, publicans whose pubs did not have a dartboard found that their public bar customers migrated to a neighbouring hostelry where they could find a game.

To prevent this mass exodus various schemes were devised to accommodate a dartboard. Smaller public houses had major problems some of which were overcome by declaring a shorter length of oche (perhaps as close as 6ft) or allowing players to have a throwing area which dissected the bar where games had to pause while customers came in or out.

The most bizarre adjustment was found in The Case is Altered pub near Ruislip where, because of the low ceiling, the landlord had to dig a little pit in the floor which the players had to stand in to ensure that the board was at the correct height.

As recently as 1973, when the second darts boom began, a Cornish publican decided to add darts to the attractions available at his pub but the pub ceiling was only 5ft 10in high. To overcome this he hung the dartboard as high up the wall as he could and then dug a trench in the bar floor for the players to stand in.

That same year Stan Timms, landlord of the Plough Inn at West Hanney, North Berkshire, had similar problems. During games darts would become embedded in the very low ceiling of Stan's thatched and timbered pub. To solve the problem Stan dug a trench 10ft long, 6in deep and 3ft across. The construction included a 45-degree slope at the entrance to prevent players from tripping into or out of the trench.

YOUR NUMBERS ARE UP

Not bothering to standardise their lotto numbers selection and play the same numbers every week, a syndicate of eleven friends in Newcastle-under-Lyme, Staffordshire, used darts. Wherever the darts landed, those six numbers would be used.

Unscientific? Yes, perhaps, but this method did scoop the group £1,113,653 (that's £101,241 each) in a September 2003 draw.

HIGH DARTERS

On Shrove Tuesday in the year 2000 after some of the team had accidently devoured home-made cakes laced with 'magic mushrooms' at an earlier venue, a Caerphilly darts team went to their away game at Llanharry in the Glamorgan Super League.

When the team was 3–1 up and seemingly in control the drug began to take effect and eventually the game had to be abandoned. The captain of the Caerphilly team said, 'My team just started going down like ninepins. One minute we were winning 3–1 and confident of victory, the next it all started to go wrong . . . It was really weird. They started laughing and giggling and some burst into tears. They were falling down, sitting on the floor and just acting plain stupid.'

Four of the team were OK as they had not eaten the cakes but three players with heart conditions were admitted to the local hospital.

THE WINMAU WORLD MASTERS

The Winmau World Masters is the longest-running major darts tournament. Winners, runners-up and venues can be found in other darts books and online but here the origins of the tournament are traced and recorded in book form for the first time together with details of how this led to the Winmau Dartboard Company and the British Darts Organisation (BDO) working together for approaching four decades to bring the very best of world darts (men's, women's, boys' and girls') to fans and players throughout the world.

EDDIE'S IDEA

In 1973 darts organiser and entrepreneur Eddie Norman had successfully run the first Home International Darts Championship in Bristol. At that time the popularity of darts was advancing rapidly across the UK but slowly across the world. The key question was how to interest the rest of the planet in the sport of darts.

In September that same year Eddie was flying back from New York after a business trip, meeting Bob McLeod, of the United States Darts Association. Bob also organised the annual United States Open.

Eddie was sitting in the plane, relaxing and daydreaming about how darts could possibly grow into an international sport when he thought of the idea of a 'World Masters' of darts, hoping that enough players from overseas could be found to make it look like a proper world darts event.

But Eddie's idea, however good it was, would never be a success unless a sponsor could be secured and this was the early 1970s and potential sponsors were very thin on the ground. Darts still had a low media profile.

INVOLVING THE WORLD

When Eddie returned home he sounded out a number of his darts contacts across the world. Tom Fleetwood, a darts organiser in California, was contacted and as a result formed an American darts organisation focusing on the West Coast from which a player would be drawn for the tournament. Then Bob McLeod got wind of the event and immediately wanted to send a representative from the East Coast.

Eddie contacted Patric Eneroth and Kent Seagren who were heavily involved with darts in Sweden and they agreed to arrange a play-off to decide the Swedish entry. Things were progressing well. The interest was there and all that was needed was organisational resources and financial backing.

Back at home in the UK two great darts characters Frank Quinn, Chairman of the Scottish Darts Association, and Louis Donohoe, who ran the All Ireland Darts Association, became involved and produced Scottish and Irish play-offs to enable those countries to send representatives to the tournament.

THE BDO COMES ON BOARD

Back in 1973, Eddie approached the head of the BDO, Olly Croft, and they discussed the World Masters proposal. Once Olly was on board he knew they had a winner. According to Eddie, Olly and his wife Lorna were the 'dream team' to have to help launch the World Masters (or any tournament for that matter).

SECURING SPONSORSHIP

With planning well and truly underway, the next major tasks were to secure a sponsor and decide on a venue. While a sponsor was being sought, it was agreed to stage the event at the West Centre Hotel, Fulham. The hotel was booked amid promises that they would get their money back on drinks.

As for a sponsor, West of England BDO Council members Ken Nicholas and Bill Sheppard agreed that if one could not be found in time then they would each put up £200 to ensure that the event went ahead. Eddie said, 'That may not seem much but it was a lot of money in those days.' However, in the end Ken and Bill's offer was not required as the record company Phonogram offered to sponsor the event. The company, which had such famous and diverse artistes on their books as Status Quo, Nana Mouskouri, Harry Secombe and Rod Stewart, agreed to put up £400 and also supply the hit-making duo of the day, Peters and Lee, as the cabaret.

THE LINE-UP AND SELL-OUT

With everything in place, the date for the inaugural World Masters Individual Darts Championship was set as Saturday 31 August 1974; a historic day for darts. The first darters toed the hockey (as it was spelt then) at 12.30 p.m.

The twenty-two man line-up comprised of (in alphabetical order): Joseph Baltadonis (USA), John Bassett (England), John Craine (Isle of Man), Andre Declerq (Belgium), Duncan Dinnie (Scotland), Dalys Elias (Wales), William Glassey (Isle of Man), Joseph Goodwin (Gibraltar), Harry Heenan (Scotland), Clifford Inglis (England), John Kellard (England), George Lee (England), Barry Luckham (England), Joseph McKenna (Ireland), Douglas Melander (Sweden), Ceri Morgan (Wales), Seamus O'Brien (Ireland), Charles Pitchers (England), Douglas Preistner (England), Jody Simpkins (USA), Ronald Stouchbury (England) and Frederick Turner (England); champions all.

The tournament was a sell-out (not surprising when you learn that a ticket cost a mere 40p) and ticket-holding darts fans were queuing outside the West Centre Hotel three hours before the event. According to *Darts World* magazine the standard of darts was 'in the most cases exceptional with many of the relative 'unknowns' giving good account of themselves.' Two of the best known players, England's Cliff Inglis and Scotland's Harry Heenan, met in the close-fought best of five legs final with Inglis just edging out Heenan 3–2 to become the first 'Darts Master of the World'. Cliff collected the winner's cheque for £400 and '£200 worth of equipment'.

Eddie Norman said recently, 'This was the first World Darts event and spectators and players had smelt darts blood and they wanted more.' Little did Eddie know that the event he thought up on a plane in 1973 and financed on a shoestring would still be fought for by top darters from across the world nearly four decades later.

Although Phonogram sponsored the second World Masters event in 1975, they withdrew their support thereafter and the search was on for a new sponsor. The most natural place to start was the Winmau Dartboard Company; that company's dartboards being already endorsed by the BDO and were certainly used in the second World Masters, if not the first too.

THE FIRST WINMAU WORLD MASTERS

The first Winmau World Masters was held at the West Centre Hotel, London, on 20 November 1976 and featured representatives of no less than thirteen different darting nations. The inaugural Winmau World Masters was won by England's John Lowe who whitewashed Wales' Phil Obbard 3–0 in the final to earn the title and collect the £1,000 winner's cheque. As if to reinforce the true international status of the event and to show how the sport was spreading across the globe, the losing semi-finalists were Javier Gopar (USA) and the Australian darter, Kevin White.

Thereafter the international reputation of the Winmau World Masters surged, achieving everything that Eddie Norman and the BDO had hoped. The Winmau company's association with this prestigious tournament has continued up to the present day. From small enthusiastic beginnings and a men's winning cheque of £400, the Winmau, as it is now commonly known, became the richest two-day tournament on British TV when it offered top prize for the Men's Masters Champion in 2007 of £25,000.

MAJOR RULE CHANGE

In the first ever Winmau World Masters in 1976 players from thirteen countries had participated from a standing start. This meant that all players had to play in the first round, the seeds mingling with the non-seeds from the very start. For over 30 years this system worked extremely well with, usually, a 'name' lifting the title. Despite this, in 2007 a major rule change was introduced following a decision made by BBC TV which ensured that the top names were present during the televised stages. Basically this meant that the top eight seeds progressed automatically through to the last sixteen, while the other eight places were taken up by players who had fought their way through via the traditional route of board finals, through to group finals then to stage finals.

Many traditionalists saw this action as not only giving the eight seeds a clear advantage over the other eight finalists (which it obviously did) but also as devaluing the tournament. However, the viewing figures seemed to support the BBC's decision when it was revealed that the average viewing figures for the two-day World Masters event were 1.2 million for the Saturday (peaking at 1.6 million) and 1.5 million for the Sunday, peaking at 1.9 million (the latter figure representing a 12.8 per cent share of the available audience) for the final between Scotland's Robert Thornton and England's Darryl Fitton staged at Leisure World, Bridlington, West Yorkshire. In 2012 the rule was changed again, this time the top sixteen seeds going straight through to the stage finals.

RECORD BREAKERS

For the record Eric Bristow triumphed in the World Masters on five occasions, 1977 (beating Paul Reynolds), 1979 (beating Allan Hogg), 1981 (John Lowe), 1983 (Mike Gregory) and 1984 (Keith Deller). Bob Anderson and Martin Adams are the only players to retain their title at the first time of asking, Anderson in 1987 and 1988, Adams in 2008 and 2009.

Bob Anderson was the first to achieve 'three-in-a-row' when he lifted the title again in 1989. Anderson had beaten Canadian Bob Sinnaeve in the 1987 final and then overcame John Lowe in the finals of 1988 and 1989. Martin Adams achieved his hat-trick in 2010 when he beat England's Stuart Kellett in the final. His 2008 and 2009 victories were over Scott Waites and Robbie Green respectively. But again hardened traditionalists viewed Adams' three victories as hollow as he, like the other seven seeds, merely had to sit and wait to see who they would face in the last sixteen as the non-seeds fought their way from board, to floor to stage.

In 2011 the BBC withdrew from televising the Winmau and cable network ESPN took over. Although no official viewing figures were available a BDO spokesman said, 'This was their [ESPN's] first foray into televised darts and they were more than happy with the audiences it attracted.'

FASCINATING DARTS DRINKING FACT

On the Saturday of the Winmau World Masters held at the City Hall, Hull, in November 2010 darts fans exceeded themselves by drinking the place dry of draught beer and lager. A barmaid was heard to say, 'I told 'em. I said these were good drinkers but would they listen?'

Fortunately supplies were replenished in time for the finals on Sunday.

IT'S CRICKET BUT IT'S NOT . . .

One of the fascinating things about the game of darts is that so many alternative games can be played on a standard dartboard, thus providing a break from the usual game of 501 while at the same time affording the players time for a bit of fun while requiring no less skill.

UK darters have a passion for playing alternative games and over the years have devised a number that have their roots in other sports and games, including bowls, football, golf, shove ha'penny and brag. Other popular games devised in the past have included Shanghai, Tactics, Halve it and Round the Board. There are many, many others including one devised by Jabez Gotobed in the late 1970s called Marilyn Monroe.

ECCENTRICITY

Typical of the Brits we've seen eccentricity too and the king of this aspect of alternative darts must surely be Steve Watton who in the mid-1980s invented some new games because he believed that '501 can be too serious for practice darts'. In his 1986 publication *Darts – Amazing New Games* Steve featured new ideas including the introduction of playing cards which allowed 'the most amazing games to be conceived.' These included Pontoon Darts and Darts Rummy but the most complicated was Jason and the Argonauts where playing cards were included as Fortune Cards to assist the darts players to find the Golden Fleece.

However, the most amazing game must surely have been Jumbo Landing in which a pack of cards was not required but a large table certainly was, 'preferably 4ft long'. In this game players utilised the dartboard as the Control Panel and the darts as the Flying Instructions. The first player to successfully land their jumbo jet on the dining room table was the winner!

CRICKET

One of the most popular alternative darts games in the UK is, not surprisingly, Cricket based of course on the noble game. In brief, two equal teams of two or more players are selected. Ten 'wickets' are chalked on the scoreboard and, after tossing a coin to decide which team throws first, the game begins, one member of the bowling team throwing first, followed by one of the batting team and so on.

The aim for the batting team is to score 41 points or more with each throw. Everything over 40 points counts as score. For the bowling team every outer bull scores one wicket, while every bull's-eye counts as two wickets. However, the bowlers must be careful not to hit any number outside of the treble ring. If they do then the value of what they hit is credited to the batting side.

Scores are accumulated on the scoreboard and each wicket is wiped off as they are hit. When all ten wickets have fallen, the sides change roles. The team with the highest score at the end of the innings is the winner.

IT'S NOT CRICKET BUT IT IS . . .

In the USA one of *the* most popular darts games, often exceeding the popularity of 501, is 'Cricket'. However, this has nothing whatsoever to do with the English sport or the UK darts version of it.

In US 'Cricket' the aim is to accrue the highest possible score while at the same time making it difficult for the opposing team to score points. Players achieve this by opening (also know as 'owning') and closing the numbers 20, 19, 18, 17, 16, 15 and both the inner and outer bull's-eye.

Those numbers are chalked vertically on a scoreboard and each member of the opposing teams tries to hit the designated numbers. In order to 'open' a number the players must hit the chosen number three times and this can be done by hitting singles, singles and a double, or a treble. Once the three strikes are registered then players in that team (and that team only) can begin to score on that number. Cumulative scores for each team are recorded on the scoreboard.

Scoring is all-important but tactics are important too; watching what the opponent has opened and closed and what strategy is best to ensure you win the game. Closing all the numbers does not necessarily mean victory. Only the team with the highest score at the end when all numbers have been closed or are 'owned' by one team wins.

Keen alternative game fans reading this might well say, 'Hey! That's not cricket. That's 'Tactics'!' and yes, they'd be right. US Cricket was originally called Tactics over here in the UK and in some places inexplicably called 'Mickey Mouse'. But whatever it is called, this is one of the most adversarial of alternative dart games. It is an intriguing and strategic game, best played with teams rather than one individual competing against another.

In the US they take the game so seriously that in 1986 top American darter Tony Payne wrote the series called 'Thermonuclear Cricket' for *Bull's-Eye News* [BEN]. In the March/April 2008 issue of *BEN*, due to popular demand, Payne's series was relaunched. Including chapters titled 'Cricket Primer', 'Picking the best first shot', 'Slaying Dragons' and 'The Comeback Counterattack', the series continued to be featured in *BEN* in 2012, showing just how serious our darting friends across the big pond take their 'Cricket'.

WHY 'CRICKET'?

It is obvious why Cricket in the UK is called Cricket; because it resembles the game of cricket. But why is Tactics called Cricket in the USA?

One theory was that while playing various alternative games in English pubs in the Second World War an American serviceman who had enjoyed playing both Tactics and Cricket but preferred the former went home, confused the titles and called Tactics Cricket.

In *Dr Darts' Newsletter* (issue no. 2 March/April 2010 and no. 3 May 2010) the mystery was practically solved. The first theory was from writer and author Mat Coward who said:

It's often forgotten that cricket was the national sport of north America for a long time - certainly long enough for some of its terms to have entered the language (and subsequently lingered). In fact, there's a surprising amount of cricket played over there even now. I think it tends to be invisible, simply because in the US . . . it's not (over there) a big money game (so no TV coverage).

The second response was from Jay Tomlinson, the editor of *Bull's-Eye News*, with his own theory. He wrote:

I just finished reading your *Newsletter* and got a kick out of the Cricket theories. My take is that your initial thought is correct in that US military persons stationed in England played both darts (tactics) and cricket. I don't believe when they returned they confused the name of the game though. I believe that the American dart game is called Cricket because it has a bit of similar nomenclature.

I have often heard the term 'innings' referred to in darts as the needs to close the six numbers and the bull's-eye. For instance, there are seven innings in cricket. There are three 'marks' needed to close a number in cricket (tactics) and there are three stumps to a wicket in cricket. There are other similar comparisons to the terms used as scoring, outs, etc, but it's still a bit of a stretch.

Bottom line, you're right, most Americans haven't a clue how English Cricket is played!

So it wasn't another example of them taking one of our games and messing it about.

UNKNOWN WADDELL

Probably *the* greatest darts commentator of all time and with an uncanny ability to bend the English language to suit, 'The Voice of Darts', the legendary Sid Waddell, was accused of destroying the Queen's English and even making the former Formula One motor racing commentator Murray Walker sound reserved.

His vocal mannerisms, for the BBC and from 1994 to 2012 for the WDC/PDC, have been compared with 'the noise a foghorn makes out at sea' and the speed of his delivery earned him the occasional moniker 'Motormouth'. Also known as the 'Geordie lip' and 'The Picasso of the palpitating prose', this working-class icon continues to be worshipped by darts fans around the world (although not totally understood in some countries).

Mike Walters, darts correspondent for the *Daily Mirror,* summed up Sid's appeal when he wrote, 'If puns, pathos or peerless analogy is your currency, nobody does it better.' Of his own drive and determination Sid told Mike before the 2007 PDC World Darts Championship at the Circus Tavern in Purfleet, Essex, 'I've got a degree in patter and I'll be using every trick in the book to keep it bright and brash.'

He never failed to deliver.

Even when Sid was fighting to cure his lost voice with 'salt shandies' (warm water and salt taken three times a day) in time for the start of the 2005 Premier League he told the *People*, rather reservedly, 'We're not used to drinking shandy in darts, but it's not half working!'

When asked what after 35 years in the darts commentary box his proudest moment was he responded, 'Being voted Sports Commentator of the Year in 2002 by seventy-five other sports commentators.'

In January 2008 Sid and his long-time darts commentary colleague, the equally legendary Dave Lanning, were inducted into the PDC Hall of Fame in recognition of their contributions to darts over 30 years of broadcasting. Sid and Dave had first worked together back in 1973 on *The Indoor League* for Yorkshire Television.

FAMOUS UTTERANCES

Avid darts fans will be familiar with Sid's more popular utterances the most well-known of which include 'There hasn't been this much excitement since the Romans fed the Christians to the lions', 'That's the greatest comeback since Lazarus' and his most famous 'There's only one word for that – Magic Darts'. Such quotes can be found in many darts and non-darts books and on numerous websites but for the most comprehensive listing go to Sid's own website www.sidwaddell.com, click on 'Sid's Classics'.

However, presented here is a selection of Sid's wise words of wisdom which have been gathered from sources ranging from obscure and relatively unknown darts magazines through national newspapers to Sid's own written work.

So here's Sid on . . .

The Origins of Darts

'When the troglodytes weren't dragging their cavewomen about by their hair or hunting meat for brontosaurus butties, their favourite pastime was throwing flint axes at a target.'

1975

Anne Boleyn's gift of dartes to King Henry VIII

'Maybe if she had stuck to plain tungsten Henry would have not been so eager to call on the axe-man.'

1979

Jocky Wilson

'Jocky almost breathes aggression on the oche. You expect him at any time to pull a skean-dhu from his stocking top and brandish it at the crowd.'

On Jocky as one of Sid's 'Eight to Watch' in 1979

John 'Old Stoneface' Lowe

'Lowe's thoroughness is legendary in the game. He approaches top darts the way Rommel approached desert warfare.'

Bedside Darts, 1985

A throw too far?

'There are those who reckon it [darts] has no place in yuppie society. But I think they've gone overboard in cleaning it up. Darts is about pints, fags and blokes in cardigans.'

The *Observer,* January 1990

Lowe versus Lazarenko

'John's been rolling like the breakers in the Atlantic while Cliff's like the fisherman, trying to hold back the waves. The question is, which way will the tide go?'

The Dart Age magazine, 1991

Darts becoming an Olympic sport

'If they can [agree] little girls with their legs sticking out of the water [darts] can.'

CDO darts magazine, 1994

Women's Darts

'It's like watching paint dry.'

CDO darts magazine, 1994

About Cliff Lazarenko

'He's the biggest tosser I've ever met in me life!'

CDO darts magazine, 1994

Being the voice of the lottery

'I was supposed to drive a lorry around the country with the balls machine in it and we would do the draw somewhere different every week. I couldn't drive the lorry, so I ended up reading the numbers in a shed. I was fired after one show.'

TV & Satellite Week

On sex

'Darts has been sexy since we discovered Velcro and superflock. Alan Evans turned up in 1976 in a white spandex Elvis suit with leeks attached to it and had the ladies going mad . . .'

Daily Express, December 2007

Colin 'The Wizard' Osborne

'I've seen more fat on a jockey's whip.'

TV & Satellite Week

James 'The Machine' Wade

'Sometimes he seems like a man who's woken up in a thick fog.'

TV & Satellite Week

Even when he transferred from the BBC to the PDC commentary box in 1994, Sid could not resist a small pop at the then controlling force of the BDO. During his commentary on the inaugural World Matchplay at Blackpool in July that year Sid observed, 'Whether watching from Mars, at the North Pier or in your living room in Muswell Hill, you've got to admit this is top quality darts.'

DEBAGGED WADDELL

During a friendly match between a team from BBC Television and representatives of the British Darts Organisation during the Embassy World Professional Darts Championship at Jollees Cabaret Club, Stoke-on-Trent in January 1981, Sid lost his trousers. The BDO rules clearly stated 'no jeans' so when Sid appeared wearing a pair he was immediately debagged.

For once, what Sid said about this incident is unrecorded.

HOT DOGS AND HOT ROCK

It is a little-known fact that in 1961 Sid and his friend 'Bucko' were the first to set up an American hot dog stand in Cambridge. The sales cart was constructed out of old orange boxes.

Three years later in 1964 Sid appeared on national and local TV as a member of the Steaming Hot Gravy Boatmen, a singing group who wore fishermen's sweaters on stage. Following this exposure the group were booked as the top-line act at the South Bank Sports Club, Middlesbrough. Sid recalled, 'It didn't go very well. We were booed off halfway through the second number.'

THE 'VOICE' IS STILLED

On 21 September 2011 the PDC issued a statement from Dick Allix, Sid's manager, which confirmed that following tests, Sid had been diagnosed with bowel cancer. The news shocked the darts world and for some months the Sky commentary box fell relatively silent as Sid took time out to battle the disease.

Never a quitter, Sid came through the treatment and eventually rejoined the Sky commentary team. His first commentary back in business was on the opening night of the McCoy's Premier League Darts at the Manchester Arena in February 2012, where he commentated on the opening match between Andy 'The Hammer' Hamilton and James 'The Machine' Wade.

But his return to the commentary box was only temporary. Sadly, the cancer returned and after a brave battle against his condition, Sid died on Saturday 11 August 2012. The world of darts mourned a true genius.

IF MUSIC BE THE FOOD OF DARTS . . .

In March 2012 Chas Hodges (one half of Chas & Dave) announced that he and his band were to record a charity single and that they were linking up with Premier League stars Gary Anderson, Andy Hamilton, Adrian Lewis, Kevin Painter, Phil Taylor, Raymond van Barneveld, James Wade and Simon Whitlock to record the video of the single which would also include walk-on girl Jacqui Adams.

The song was released exclusively on iTunes on Friday 18 May 2012 after being premiered at the McCoy's Premier League play-offs at the O2 in London. All proceeds went to the Haven House Children's Hospice.

But, of course, this is not the first time darts players have appeared on video or, perish the thought, even stood behind a microphone and sung!

NOT SINGING

When the rock band The Darkness came to prominence in 2003 it was revealed by lead singer Justin Hawkins that he loved the sport of darts, that he had a 'darts shrine' at home and that Phil Taylor was one of his idols. Justin began to make appearances (in the VIP lounge) at PDC events and became friends with a number of top darters including, of course, 'The Power'.

In 2005 Hawkins branched out on a solo project and recorded the old Sparks '70s hit 'This Town Ain't Big Enough for Both of Us' under the band name British Whale. The video accompanying the song featured a darts match featuring, not surprisingly, Hawkins playing against his hero 'The Power'; a match which Hawkins won on the bull's-eye.

During that same year the *Sun* revealed that Hawkins was busy devising a pro-celebrity TV darts game called 'Fame On!' where fifteen celebrities battled it out against fifteen professional darts players. He said at the time, 'I'm talking to various darts pros and we'll get it made before the end of the year.'

SINGING

Described as 'The combine harvester-driving legends of the West Country', the Wurzels are probably best known for their 1976 number one hit 'Combine Harvester' (a parody of Melanie Safka's song 'Brand New Key'). The album spawned by that hit, cleverly titled 'The Combine Harvester', included the song 'Middle for Diddle' which told of the gamesmanship which needed to be employed during a darts match to make sure your team wins.

Alan Smethurst, better known as 'The Singing Postman' and famous for the hit 'Hev yew gotta loight boy' always wrote his songs about everyday things and everyday people. Many, such as 'They're Orl Playin' Dommies in the Bar' were based upon Smethurst's visits to pubs across Norfolk. In 1966 Parlophone records released a new single 'Roundabout'. The 'B' side was titled 'The Ladies Darts Team'.

SINGING DARTERS

In 1981 Smile records released the song '180!' the official BDO theme tune for the British Darts Team. The featured darts players were Bobby George, Jocky Wilson, Angus Ross, Kevin White, Tony Sontag and Gordon Allpress. 'The Caller' was Freddie Williams and the backing group, the BDO Choir, included Olly Croft and Freddie's wife Pat.

THE DART SONG

The earliest recorded song about darts is 'The Dart Song' written by 1930s variety artist and songwriter Leslie Sarony. It was especially commissioned by the *News of the World* to celebrate its darts competition and Sarony recorded it with the Jack Hylton Orchestra in London. It was released on His Master's Voice records on 23 April 1937.

Sarony also released a recording of the song with Leslie Holmes (the duo being called 'The Two Leslies'), another version also being recorded by Billy Cotton and his band on Rex Records the same year.

TOBY TWIRL

In 1981 it was rumoured that singer Dudley Doolittle, an enthusiastic pub darts player who worked the northern clubs as a member of the comedy group Toby Twirl and the Pickwicks, had turned solo and, looking for his first hit, had recorded a song, '180! He's Done It Again'.

The song had been written for him by Mike Coleman, one half of the chart-topping duo Brian and Michael who had shot to fame in 1978 with their self-penned 'Matchstalk Men and Matchstalk Cats & Dogs'. However, Toby's song does not seem to have ever seen the light of day.

IN PRAISE OF PHIL

In 2004 Tony Shailer and Mike Ryde, directors of Shailer Ryde Music, wrote and produced a song called 'Phil "The Power" Taylor – Better than the best'.

Having honed their product and keen to have Phil's approval and support of the project, discussions were being planned in 2007 but it is unclear if the project ever took off.

SINGING TOURNAMENT DIRECTOR

In September 2001 the PDC Tournament Director Dick Allix appeared on BBC TV's pop music quiz show *Never Mind the Buzzcocks*. Dick told the PDC website that he would be 'making an arse' of himself in the section of the show where former pop stars, now getting on in years, have to be picked from an identity parade following the teams seeing an old video clip.

Dick cut his pop teeth with a band called the Gnomes of Zurich but found fame in the 1970s as a member of Vanity Fare who had such top hits as 'Hitchin' A Ride', 'I Live for the Sun' and 'Early in the Morning'.

RELEASE ME, LET ME GO

Forget about the result of the 2012 Eurovision Song Contest – think back to the 1990s when singer Engelbert Humperdinck trounced the best darts players backstage at a Las Vegas casino. Engelbert is a great fan of darts.

Eric Bristow, Mike Gregory, Jamie Harvey, Cliff Lazarenko, John Lowe, Dennis Priestley and Jocky Wilson were among the audience at the star's cabaret show. Engelbert invited them to a backstage bash where he challenged each and every one to a game of darts. According to Jocky Wilson, 'He beat each of us at least once.'

In 1973 Engelbert and fellow mega-star and darts fanatic Tom Jones met for a game of darts at a mock English pub in Sacramento. The match was arranged by Ted Hickman, a Sacramento Chamber of Commerce official when Engelbert and Tom found that they were appearing in cabaret within 200 miles of each other.

Tom travelled from San Francisco and Engelbert from Lake Tahoe for the match which Ted Hickman said was 'to settle [the] question about the fishing rights on a 3,000-acre ranch they had purchased recently.' Hickman added, 'They called me, and I set it all up, with genuine English dartboards sent in from London.'

Although Engelbert won the singles match, the fishing rights were determined by a team game which Tom's team won 2–1.

DARTS MYTHOLOGY

'BIGFOOT' ANNAKIN PROVED THAT DARTS WAS A GAME OF SKILL

The court case in Leeds involving a man named Annakin in 1908 is part myth and part truth. It is the case that, apparently, made darts a legal pub pastime. However, over time the fragments of actual truth have become distorted and the story and its importance blown out of all proportion.

THE PART-MYTH

One day in 1908 William 'Bigfoot' Annakin, a Leeds publican, stood before Leeds Magistrates' Court to answer a charge of allowing a game of chance, namely darts, to be played in his establishment. Annakin duly turned up at court clutching a Yorkshire Board and, needing little encouragement from officials, set about proving that darts was a game of skill.

He did this by first landing three darts in the single twenty segment. The magistrate then asked the clerk of the court to throw three darts, only one of which actually hit and stayed in the dartboard. Annakin then strode up and thudded three darts out of three into double top. The magistrate was duly impressed and announced without further evidence that 'This is no game of chance. Case dismissed!'

From then, it is claimed, darts became legal and from henceforth publicans celebrated and darts was never to be illegal again.

What a load of tosh!

DARTS IN 1908

At the turn of the twentieth century darts was in its infancy in England. However, the attractions of the public house or beerhouse were not merely the games played there, like darts, crib or dominoes. Drunkenness was a curse of the working class and men came to the pub not only to imbibe but to gamble away the few pennies they had. Pub games were inextricably linked with gaming – playing for money or money's worth – and as a result were looked upon by the local authorities, the police and licensing justices as encouraging 'ne'er do wellism'. To this end, the Gaming Acts were clear and records reveal the many hundreds of licensees who were brought before the courts to answer charges of allowing gaming on their premises.

As far as the more enlightened authorities were concerned, the playing of games of skill was allowed, provided it was not directly linked with gaming. Darts became more popular during the early Edwardian period and spread from its origins in the south to the Midlands and the north. There some justices found difficulty in determining whether darts was a game of chance – and therefore illegal – or a game of skill and therefore legal. Magistrates in Leeds took up the cudgel. The man credited with taking on the law of the land and winning was William 'Bigfoot' Annakin.

THE FABRICATION AND THE TRUTH

The facts in the case of William Annakin are never consistent and it would seem that every darts writer who has ever put pen to paper about this important legal case has added a little embellishment of his own. However, recent research has revealed the following . . .

The man in question, William 'Bigfoot' Annakin was not a publican at all. He worked at a forge in Kirkstall Road, Leeds. Annakin was actually the best darts and dominoes player in the Adelphi Inn, a beerhouse near to his place of work. When the landlord of the Adelphi, Jim Garside, was summoned to Leeds Magistrates' Court to answer the charge of allowing a game of chance to be played on his premises, what better tactic than to take along the best darter you have?

Annakin's grandson revealed in 1986 that there was no drama in the courtroom involving the clerk of the court. He said, 'My grandfather was not a publican but the best darts player around at the time and the landlord of the Adelphi got him to go to court to prove darts was a game of skill. The JPs [Justices of the Peace] asked him to place the darts in selected numbers and he duly obliged, proving it was a game of skill.'

One published version of the court 'drama' tells of 'Bigfoot' shooting three treble twenties to impress the bench. That would have been *very* impressive as the dartboard Garside took with him was a Yorkshire Board which did not have a treble ring.

So 'Bigfoot' Annakin left his mark on the history of darts. Unfortunately, apart from his grandson's oral testimony, it is impossible to prove that the court case ever took place. There are no reports of the case in any of the local newspapers published in 1908 and surprisingly the actual records of the Leeds Magistrates Court for that year were, unaccountably, lost.

DARTS AND THE OLYMPICS

The 2012 London Olympic Games have come and gone and darts was not there, not even as a demonstration sport.

No chance then for a men's darts 'Team GB', comprising Phil Taylor (England, captain), Gary Anderson (Scotland), Mark Webster (Wales) and Brendan Dolan (Northern Ireland), to bring home gold medals. No opportunity for the ladies' darts 'Team GB', comprising Trina Gulliver (England, captain), Julie Gore (Wales), Robyn McCloy (Scotland) and Denise Cassidy (Northern Ireland) to strut their stuff and step up on to the victory rostrum and wave to an enthusiastic home crowd.

NO PROTEST

Those disappointed that one of the most popular sporting activities in Britain failed to find a place in the Olympics have not been very vocal. There was no mass petition and only a few bursts of opinion on various blogs where, in general, those in favour of recognition ('Darts is a proper sport, just try playing it and you will quickly appreciate the skill level involved') *just* outnumbered those who were against it ('No way . . . Definitely no place for darts in my eyes').

'WOLFIE' EXPLAINS

Three-time world title holder Martin 'Wolfie' Adams pointed out in January 2009 that sports for the London 2012 games were decided by the International Olympic Committee (IOC) in 2005. He stated, 'The London 2012 Organising Committee is not involved in these decisions although we take great interest in the results.' Darts was not formally recognised as a sport by the UK Sports Councils until mid-2005 so it has to be assumed that whatever representations the British Darts Organisation made to the IOC before or after then for darts to become a demonstration sport were either too early or too late.

NOW WE'RE LOOKING AT IT

Surprisingly the World Darts Federation (WDF) was not involved in that process but is now actively pursuing formal recognition for darts as an Olympic sport. At the SportAccord Annual Meeting in London in 2011, the international sport federations which are not IOC-recognised joined forces to form an 'Alliance of Sports Federations'; SportAccord being an 'umbrella organisation for all (Olympic and non-Olympic) international sports as well as organisers of multi-sports games and sport-related international associations' – motto 'Unite & Support'. From within that alliance a working group is now actively lobbying the IOC 'with the view of obtaining blanket approval.'

As this book was being completed the WDF committee were 'in active dialogue with SportAccord and the IOC'.

Some sceptics might say that this is all a little too late.

However, darts fans can seek some solace in the fact that darts has already featured in 'Olympics'.

BEEN THERE, DONE THAT – MEXICO '68

Remember Mexico in 1968?

So probably do the men of the fifteen ships (representing eight different nations) that formed a northbound convoy which had entered the Suez Canal in June 1967 and became trapped in the Great Bitter Lakes for almost eight years. In an article published in *The Review* (The Journal of the Naval Historical Collectors & Research Association), Richard Cornish revealed that in 1968 the men on those ships organised their own Olympics to correspond with those being held in Mexico.

The cause was one of the shortest wars on record, the Six-Day War between Israel and Egypt, Jordan and Syria where 'Various vessels had been sunk at both ends of the Suez Canal which made safe transit impossible' so the ships and their crews already in the canal stayed where they were.

After a degree of normality returned and communications between ships and shore, including visits, were restored, a meeting was convened of 'as many men as possible from all ships' on the British 8,509-ton *Melamus*. From this gathering the Great Bitter Lakes Association (GBLA) was formed with the object of 'promoting mutual assistance, friendships and eventually joint events.'

Richard Cornish revealed that some of the first 'events' were darts competitions 'with fish and chip suppers' on the British ships. At a meeting of the GBLA in 1968 it was decided to hold its own version of the Olympics to coincide with the official world event in Mexico.

The eight nations represented were Britain, America, Poland, Sweden, Czechoslovakia, West Germany, France and Bulgaria. The teams competed in fourteen events (the number of ships trapped in the canal). Games included sailing, swimming, fishing, air-rifle shooting, long jump, high jump, gymnastics, five-a-side football and darts.

Although who actually won the 'Olympics' that year on the Suez Canal is not recorded, Richard's research shows that a badge and certificate was presented to everyone who participated in 'the Games'. The little badge, which bears the legend 'OLYMPIC GAMES 1968 GBLA', was 'designed and manufactured through the efforts of the two German ships'. The badge has since become a great rarity.

THE OLYMPIC STAMPS OF APPROVAL

Despite darts never being featured in any Olympic Games, this did not prevent a couple of overzealous countries from producing celebratory Olympic postage stamps featuring the sport.

In 1964 (the year of the Tokyo Olympics) the Yemen Arab Republic produced a stamp showing a man throwing darts at a concentric (miniature archery) target. Later, in 1992 (when the Olympic Games were held in Spain), Tanzania issued a 400s stamp featuring two darts players. The design of this stamp showed a 'standard' dartboard but with a huge bull's-eye and numbering that had the number eight segment at the top of the board where the twenty segment should be.

Clearly, in one respect at least, Yemen and Tanzania were way, way ahead of their time.

How long will it actually be before Her Majesty the Queen (or more likely King Charles or maybe even King William V) looks down from the right-hand corner of one of our very expensive postage stamps, casting an admiring glance at a game of darts?

BLACK COUNTRY OLYMPICS, 1983

The cheers went up for the Sandwell team as they beat all-comers in the darts discipline during the 1983 Black Country Olympics held in July that year.

In a powerful display the team, which included members of the West Midlands county darts squad, defeated Wolverhampton in the final and was awarded 'four premium points' (the equivalent to the gold medal) for their win.

Sadly these Olympics included other games at which the Sandwell representatives did not excel at so well and the team eventually took the wooden spoon position overall – that is, last place. Each member of the participating squads was presented with a special commemorative woven badge for taking part.

TOPLESS OLYMPICS

In April 1996 the *Sunday People* newspaper reported that cable television company L!VE TV was lobbying the International Olympics Committee (IOC) to have topless darts included as a demonstration sport in the 2004 Olympics.

NICKNAMES BEFORE THEIR NICKNAMES

GARY 'THE FLYING SCOTSMAN' ANDERSON

Scotland's Gary Anderson bore the nickname 'Dream Boy' for a long time and he made no secret that he was not terribly keen on it. However, a few years ago he changed it to 'The Flying Scotsman' a nickname previously borne, among other Scottish players, by Jocky Wilson.

STEVE 'THE BRONZED ADONIS' BEATON

Tony Green named Steve 'The Bronzed Adonis' during his television commentary on the Embassy World Professional Darts Championships at Lakeside in 1991. Steve had recently returned from a holiday in Tenerife. His wife Nanette said, 'We always went on holiday in December before the Embassy World Championships started, so Steve always had a sun tan.' Tony picked up on it, mentioned on TV that Steve looked like 'a bronzed Adonis' and the nickname stuck.

Even though Steve still uses the nickname today, at some stage during his career he was dubbed 'Magnum PI' because of his likeness to US actor Tom Selleck. However, this was only temporary and never took off. More recently Nanette said, 'Some people have begun calling Steve "The Marathon Man" as he started doing runs for charity.'

STEVE 'THE ORIGINAL' BROWN

Ex-pat Steve Brown, son of the late England international Ken Brown, has lived and played his darts in the USA for many years and has racked up numerous titles in both steel- and soft-tip darts. Over the past few decades he has often returned to the UK to contest major titles.

For years Steve's nickname was 'Brownie' but then another darts player came on the scene and on to the PDC circuit – another Steve Brown. To avoid any confusion the original Steve Brown decided to change his nickname to – what else? – 'The Original'.

MARK 'FLASH' DUDBRIDGE

Mark was originally dubbed 'Flash' by his my mum when he was 18 years old. Preparing to go into town one evening she looked at her son and said 'Look at flash Harry' so that nickname stuck for some time. When it came to playing the darts circuit Mark used 'Flash' as he felt that fitted into the darts scene, plus there was Queen music to suit.

Before establishing himself on the circuit, Mark had also considered 'The Brill Bristolian' and 'Mark the Marksman' but decided against them.

Mark. Good decision.

ANDY 'THE VIKING' FORDHAM

Andy says that it was Bobby George who gave him the name but it was a guy called Carl Wilkins who dressed up as a Viking at Andy's first Embassy World Championships in 1995. Andy recalls also being dubbed 'Grizzly' and 'Bluto' on occasions.

In his younger days Andy was much slimmer than he is today and was known as 'The Whippet'.

BOBBY 'THE KING OF BLING' GEORGE

Way, way back in the 1980s Bobby was dubbed 'Liberace' after he wore sparkly shirts on stage making him look just a little like the famous exuberant American pianist. As his outfits became more extravagant he earned the nickname 'Mr Glitter' but abandoned that completely, for good reason, in the mid-2000s. Now generally known as 'The King of Bling' his other nickname 'Bobby Dazzler' was used for the title of his autobiography published in 2006.

SHAUN 'NINE-DART' GREATBATCH

Before he made darting history in 2002 by hitting the first nine-darter on live television, Cambridgeshire's Shaun Greatbatch was popularly known by his county teammates and close friends as 'Big 'un'.

It was the Dutch fans, especially those who witnessed his historic perfect game, who named Shaun 'Nine-dart'.

ROD 'THE PRINCE OF STYLE' HARRINGTON

It was MC Phil Jones who, spotting how snappily Rod dressed on the oche, gave him the name 'The Prince of Style'. Back in 2009 Rod commented, 'The name came from when we first started working for Sky and they wanted to jazz the game up a bit so we all got nicknames.'

Despite Rod hating the nickname, it stuck. Rod said, 'It did put me apart from the general dart player and the run of the mill dart shirt that most wore then and still do,' adding, 'Although I still did not like the name much I got used to it and the name and dress brought me in a lot of work that perhaps other dart players did not get offered.'

Rod originally wanted to use the nickname that Bob Anderson used to call him – 'The Rocket' – a name adopted by Ronnie Baxter.

JAMIE 'BRAVEDART' HARVEY

Massively popular on the darts scene for many years and one of the original 'rebels' who transferred their allegiance to the World Darts Council in 1993, Jamie was given the nickname 'Bravedart' by Sky.

Before that Jamie was nicknamed 'The Tartan Terror'. In 1992 Jamie played in his first Embassy World Professional Darts Championship at the Lakeside Country Club. He recalled recently, 'I wore a pair of tartan trousers and tartan shirt. I won my first game [against Finland's Heikki Hermunen 3–0] to get to the last 16. The next day I had a big spread in the *Sun* and at the top of the page was the headline 'THE TARTAN TERROR' and the nickname stuck.'

The change of nickname came during the World Cup Pairs played at Butlins, Ayr, in 1995. Jamie and pairs partner Keith Deller had beaten the pairing of Phil Taylor and Jocky Wilson so the next day Sky Sports sent Jamie to Gullane Castle, painted his face, made him wear a kilt and shot a video of him marauding through the forest like a man possessed.

In the finished product there on the screen was the legend 'BRAVEDART – THE SCOURGE OF THE ENGLISH'. 'Bravedart' was a clear reference to the highly successful film *Braveheart* starring and directed by Mel Gibson, an epic story about William Wallace, a commoner, who in the thirteenth century united the Scots in a bid to overthrow English rule.

The nickname had an immediate impact on the legion of Scottish fans at the tournament. Jamie and Keith made it to the final of the World Pairs where in front of the Scottish crowd chanting 'BRAVEDART! BRAVEDART!' they were defeated 14 legs to 9 by the English pairing of Eric Bristow and Dennis Priestley.

NIGEL 'THE UNDERTAKER' HEYDON

PDC player Nigel Heydon told reporters in 2011, 'I've been a butcher all my life until seven years ago . . . up to that point my nickname on the darts scene had been "The Butcher".'

He then changed his occupation to that of undertaker. Nigel said, 'An undertaker who's known as "The Butcher" doesn't sound great does it,' so it was a natural progression to call himself 'The Undertaker'; a man looking to 'bury' his opponents. Nigel takes to the stage with his darts in a coffin-shaped case, not unlike the prince of dartness himself, Ted Hankey.

KAREN 'LEO' LAWMAN

Just before the 2010 Lakeside Ladies' World Darts Championships Karen, who is fascinated by horoscopes, adopted the nickname 'Leo' to correspond with her birth sign. Until then Karen, the winner of the Winmau Women's World Masters in 1998 (under her married name of Smith), used to have the nickname 'Smurf'.

JOHN 'OLD STONEFACE' LOWE

This doesn't really fit the title of this section as John Lowe will answer not only to 'Old Stoneface' but also to 'Lowey' and 'Lobo' and what actually came first is likely to remain a mystery. However, his autobiography *Old Stoneface,* published in 2005, confirms the most popular nomenclature of this most popular of darts players. World Darts Champion in three different decades (1970s, 1980s and 1990s) John earned the name 'Old Stoneface' because of the fact that his face remains expressionless when he throws his darts although, as we all know, he did allow his face to crack (just a little) when he hit the first televised nine-darter at Slough in 1984.

WAYNE 'HAWAII 501' MARDLE

When Wayne Mardle first burst loudly upon the darts scene he soon became known as 'The Mouth from the South' but then he started to wear bright Hawaiian shirts in tournaments and he became more popularly known as 'Hawaii 501'.

Bobby George takes credit for giving Wayne that nickname. In his book *Scoring for Show, Doubles for Dough* Bobby wrote, 'Wayne was impressed with all my glitter and bling . . . then he decided to do a bit of that too and started walking on stage wearing a bright Hawaiian shirt to the theme of *Hawaii Five-O*. During an interview I had with Wayne I said, "You should put a '1' on the end of that so it's Hawaii 501."'

JOHN 'DARTH MAPLE' PART

Darts fans are familiar with the three-time World Champion, Canada's John Part walking on to Darth Vader's music from the *Star Wars* films and his moniker 'Darth Maple'.

John decided to adopt the nickname about the time that *Star Wars – Episode One* was released. The movie featured a character called Darth Maul. John told fans, 'The black maple leaf on my shirt, which I first wore at the 1994 Embassy, is the original Darth Maple. Dart(h) was an easy first name to pick to make the Maple ominous but all firmly tongue-in-cheek.'

But before 'Darth Maple', John had two other nicknames. He said, 'I was introduced on stage as "The Mountie" by MC Martin Fitzmaurice in the Embassy days but that was just too obvious and corny for my liking and was never going to work in Canada.'

John's very first nickname back in 1989/90 when he was playing in his first darts team was 'John the Bomb'.

PHIL 'THE POWER' TAYLOR

It was Sid Waddell who admits to dubbing Phil Taylor 'The Crafty Potter' as a substantial nod in the direction of Phil's mentor Eric 'The Crafty Cockney' Bristow. As success followed success the time came to change his nickname and what else could it be but 'The Power'?

In his autobiography *The Power – My Autobiography* Phil admitted modestly that 'The Power' was better than being referred to as 'Eric's sidekick'.

JAMES 'THE MACHINE' WADE

Aldershot's James Wade has admitted in the past that he is not a great fan of nicknames but despite this the records show that he has actually had four since he turned professional. Initially he was known as 'The Gladiator' and then soon afterwards '009'. For some reason after that nickname was dropped there followed a short period where he had no nickname at all and then the fans dubbed him 'Spectacular'.

Early 2008 saw him introduce 'The Machine' for the first time and that stuck. However, close friends usually call him 'Wadey'.

TONY 'TORNADO' WEST

Just before the final of the 2002 Winmau World Masters Tony changed his nickname to 'The Tornado' as he felt that better suited his very fast throwing style and, as Tony is quoted as saying, 'When I came on to the scene in 2002 I just blew everyone away winning so many titles and beating top players of the world. Just like a tornado, it happened so fast.' Runner-up in the Winmau World Masters in 2002, Tony lifted the title in 2003.

DAVE 'THE QUIET MAN OF DARTS' WHITCOMBE

Never one to say a great deal either on or off the oche, it was not therefore, surprising that because of this trait, in a sport that requires that players have nicknames, that Dave Whitcombe became known as 'The Quiet Man of Darts'.

Twice runner-up in the Embassy World Professional Darts Championship, twice World Master and winner of the 1989 News of the World Individual Darts Championship, Dave says that it was the usual suspects, either Tony Green or Sid Waddell, who gave him that nickname because 'I wasn't what you would call a "character" in those days.'

It is popularly believed that before this Dave was nicknamed 'Dracula' because he was rarely, if ever, seen about in daylight.

Untrue.

Dave says, 'Actually I wasn't called "Dracula" at all. Sid Waddell once referred to me as "Dracula" when he said I wasn't seen during the day. The name never stuck but being Sid, he mentioned it again during some of his commentaries.'

DARTS MYTHOLOGY

'HOCKEY' IS DERIVED FROM THE NAME OF AN ENGLISH BREWER

THE MYTH

Time and time again, you read on the internet and in darts books that the throw-line in darts was called the 'hockey' after a brewery based in either Dorset or Suffolk.

The standard story declares that when darts was young and rules were few and far between, some unnamed genius laid three wooden beer crates, measuring 3ft long each and belonging to the brewers S. Hockey & Sons, end to end from a position under the dartboard and thus determined the throwing distance of 9ft. From thenceforth the throw-line was called the 'hockey'.

Although this frivolous story was written by an English darts entrepreneur with a sense of humour in 1980 to entertain the readers of a tournament programme, it has become widely accepted as the true source of the word. The killer argument is that there never has been a brewery named Hockey & Sons anywhere in the UK.

The truth is much simpler.

THE TRUTH

The word 'hockey' was first used in darts in the 1920s and was borrowed from the pub game of 'Aunt Sally' where the throw-line was called 'the hockey'. Where exactly the word 'hockey' came from before that is subject to conjecture, but the most plausible and slightly disgusting theory is that it derived from the old Northern English word 'hocken' (meaning 'to spit'). Presumably the line was set simply by someone standing at a set position (in the case of darts, with his back to the wall on which the dartboard hung) and 'gobbing' a distance which was then marked out in chalk. So, the word 'hockey' was used in the earliest darts rules from the 1920s onwards and was ever thus until the 1970s until it was suddenly replaced by 'oche'.

The word 'oche' is an Old French word, the verb being 'oschier' or 'ocher', meaning to notch or to nick and was introduced into the language and rules of darts in the mid-1970s by Olly Croft of the British Darts Organisation (BDO).

'Hockey' was then consigned to history.

DARTEFACTS – THE FINAL DELVE INTO THE VAULT

APPLE DARTBOARDS

Darts memorabilia is becoming more and more collectable but one of the most collectable items has to be the Apple Corporation's dartboard which the Beatles used to give away to friends and employees.

Bearing the legend 'Apple Records' at the top and the Apple logo centred on the bullseye, one sold at auction in the late 1980s for £720. More recently in June 2010 an unused Apple dartboard in its original card box was sold by Bonhams of London for £3,600.

THE DARTBOARD FROM ANOTHER PLANET

Even some of our most famous people believe that aliens leave cryptic messages to humankind on the land in the form of corn circles. In 1993 creatures from another planet with a passion for darts tried to communicate with us by producing a corn circle in the shape of dartboard. It was left in a wheat field near Marlborough Downs Riding Stable, Rockley, close to the M4 near Swindon.

A local corn circle 'expert' suggested that the extraterrestrial beings had clearly given up trying to communicate with scientists and academics with their more complex designs and had turned their attention to 'a design recognisable by everyone on the entire planet.'

Or perhaps they were bidding to host the first 'out of this world' world professional darts championship!

IS THIS THE OLDEST DARTS JOKE?

A stranger was having a drink in a public house when one of the regulars suggested a game of darts.

When the stranger protested that he wasn't much of a hand at it, the other proposed playing for drinks, thinking he was on to a good thing. The game began and soon ended. The stranger seemed to get doubles and trebles just as he liked.

'I thought you didn't play much' said the loser as he ordered the drinks.

'I don't know, all I do is throw an occasional dart at a fly on the wall' replied the winner.

'But doesn't that make a mess of the wallpaper?' asked the man who was paying.

'Oh no!' was the reply, 'You see I only aim at their wings.'

The Brewer and Wine Merchant, September 1944

A newer joke
1st Darter: 'Did you hear that Jeff the captain of the Rose and Tulip darts team died last week?'

2nd Darter: 'No. What happened?'

1st Darter: 'He was hit by a flight.'

2nd Darter: 'No! How could that happen? Jeff's such a strong bloke.'

1st Darter: 'Apparently he was sleepwalking and wandered into the path of a 757.'

DOCTOR PHIL

In 2007 the phenomenal achievements of Phil Taylor were formally recognised by the Staffordshire University with the award to 'The Power' of an honorary doctorate.

With thirteen world championship titles under his belt at the time, Taylor donned mortar board and gown when he visited the university's graduation week Awards Village at Trentham Gardens to collect his honorary degree.

Burslem-born Taylor told the crowd that he had left school at fifteen and held down a number of jobs to make ends meet while perfecting his darts action. He told the packed audience in the Ceremony Hall, 'One teacher asked me what I wanted to be and I said an engineer. The teacher said I had no chance because I was rubbish. So I thought "Right then!" When I started winning at darts I bought a Jaguar and drove up and down past the school tooting the horn to make sure he knew.' Then he joked with the crowd, asking if he could now be admitted to the Students' Bar.

'NO IDEA WHY I DONE IT GUV.'

On 7 June 1945 a man in Southend-on-Sea was fined 10s for stealing a set of darts from a local branch of Woolworth's. In his defence his counsel told the court, 'He did not know why he did it, because he never plays darts.'

IRAN'S DARTS CAPABILITY

The Islamic Republic of Iran Darts Association (IDA) was established in August 2004 to 'To create happiness and health in our society.'

By 2008 more than 200 'Dart houses' had been set up in Iran with the co-operation of municipal and government organisation across twenty-five of the country's thirty states.

Today darts continues to thrive in Iran with more than 500,000 men, women and children playing the sport on a regular basis and more than 3,000 billiard clubs in that country are fitted out with a bristle dartboard and stand. Darts is also included in Iran's annual 'Olympiad' which is held under the auspices of the President, Deputy and Head of Physical Training Organisation of the Islamic Republic of Iran and involves forty-four different branches of sport. It is organised with the specific aim of increasing the quality and level of sportsmanship in that country and is totally funded by the Iranian Government.

A government spokesman said, 'The darts tournament was very successful and its inclusion in the Olympiad shows how popular and important the sport is becoming in our country.'

However, since the late 2000s most of the bristle dartboards in the billiard halls and sports centres have been replaced with electronic soft-tip darts machines.

TAKING HIS WORK HOME

In 1988 a security guard at a well-known department store in Bristol was discovered literally taking his work home with him. Over a period of seven years he stole an estimated 2,500 items and, instead of selling them on, stored the hoard throughout his home, in his loft, garage and greenhouse.

When the police eventually paid him a visit it took eight officers ten hours to remove the contraband from his home. The load included 120 video cassettes, four dozen boxes of candles, 474 glue sticks, 360 knife blades, 52 figurines, 100 golf balls, 15 sets of darts and two dartboards.

INFLATABLE DARTBOARD

Described by Weymouth's Trading Standards officers as 'a shameless piece of nonsense – but brilliant!' an inflatable dartboard hit the market in 2000 complete with a puncture repair kit. The shopping watchdogs believed that they had found the world's most useless present.

YOU ARE THE WEAKEST LINK

In an edition of *The Weakest Link* transmitted by BBC2 on 5 October 2004 Anne Robinson asked the question, 'This year Phil Taylor beat Kevin Painter to win his eleventh title in which game?'

The contestant replied 'Athletics'.

REBELS, DEFECTORS AND RETURNERS

During the 2012 Lakeside World Professional Darts Championship at Frimley Green it was announced that double world champ (2000 and 2009) and one of the few remaining characters in the sport, Ted 'The Count' Hankey, had defected to the PDC.

At the time Ted said, 'I had fifteen great years with the BDO and I thank them, but it's time to move on.' Fellow professional Terry 'The Bull' Jenkins was pleased to see Ted join the alternative code. He told reporters, 'I always told Ted that he should come across to the PDC . . . It's not only better money in the PDC but the quality of darts is better. Surely players should test themselves against the best players in the world and Hankey can't be knocked for wanting to do that.'

Ted looked forward to the challenges that playing on the PDC Tour presented but admitted that he needed to up his game if he was to achieve his ambition of making it into the Premier League.

Fellow defectors in January 2012 included Dean Winstanley and Steve West but there had been a steady number of players leaving the BDO ranks for some time and it all started two decades ago.

REBELS

Up until the end of 1992 the British Darts Organisation (BDO) controlled the sport of darts in Britain but at the turn of 1993 that control was effectively challenged when the World Darts Council (WDC) was formed.

The mandate of the new organisation, dated 4 January 1993, and signed by sixteen top professional darts players, read as follows:

We, the undersigned, members of the World Darts Players' Association, mandate the World Darts Council to represent us exclusively on all matters relating to the 1994 World Professional Darts Championship. In particular, we recognise the World Darts Council as the only governing body empowered to commit our participation in any darts tournaments worldwide.

The sixteen players, shortly afterwards to be dubbed 'rebels', were (in alphabetical order):

Bob Anderson
Eric Bristow
Keith Deller
Peter Evison
Ritchie Gardner
Mike Gregory
Rod Harrington
Jamie Harvey
Chrissie Johns
Cliff Lazarenko
John Lowe
Dennis Priestley
Kevin Spiolek
Phil Taylor
Alan Warriner
Jocky Wilson

Notable exceptions were top darters Leighton Rees, Bobby George and Alan Glazier who remained loyal to the BDO.

RETURNERS

Not all of the original sixteen 'rebels' stayed the course. Chrissie Johns was the first to return to the BDO fold and little was heard of the Welsh darts ace after that.

The highest profile 'returner' in the 1990s was Mike Gregory. Multi-titled Mike began his career with the World Darts Council in fine form winning that organisation's first ever tournament, the 1992 Lada UK Masters at the Talk of the East club in Norwich defeating Dennis Priestley 8–5 in the final. The following year Mike successfully defended his Masters title at the same venue beating Bob Anderson 8–6.

In 1994 Mike returned to the BDO for personal reasons but was not welcomed with open arms, many apparently believing that he was only coming back to take 'their' titles. Mike did indeed win a few major titles including the Belgium Open (twice), the Swedish Open (three times) and the Norwegian Open. But in 1996 Mike took the decision to retire from professional darts. However, during 2011 he began to play exhibitions again.

The most well-known lady 'defector' from the BDO to the PDC is Russian-born Anastasia Dobromyslova. Anastasia won the Lakeside Women's World Professional Darts Championship in 2008, beating multi-world title holder Trina Gulliver 2–0. By March she had topped the World Darts Federation (WDF) rankings and then in December 2008 it was announced that she had moved on to the PDC circuit; thus was unable to defend her title.

It is not unusual for players who had 'defected' from the BDO to the PDC to return to the BDO fold.

For example, in June 2007, on the eve of the UK Open, England's Tony 'The Viper' Eccles announced that he would be switching codes from the BDO to the PDC. At that time Tony was no. 2 in the World Darts Federation (WDF) rankings and no. 4 in the BDO rankings. When he started with the PDC he sat at position 151 in the Order of Merit but by February 2008 had climbed up to the Top 40, at no. 40.

But in 2012 Tony, for personal reasons, made the decision to return to the BDO code. More or less immediately Tony hit winning form with victory in the Scottish Open by five sets to three over England's Robbie Green at the Normandy Hotel, Renfrewshire. Returning to the BDO also meant that he was once again able to travel the circuit with his young family and compete in tournaments and play county darts alongside his partner Claire Stainsby.

Despite some success on the PDC Tour, in February 2010 it was announced that the Anastasia Dobromyslova (the 2008 Lakeside Women's World Professional Darts Champion) was returning to the BDO and the WDF. In a personal letter to the BDO Anastasia wrote:

> I am writing to you in regards to my wish to compete in the British Darts Organisation and the World Darts Federation.
>
> I think it is fair to say that in the past I haven't always received advice that was in my best interests. However, it is now my intention to fully commit to the BDO and WDF in their events and competitions.

Her successful return to the embrace of the BDO/WDF was capped in January 2012 when she won back her world title beating Deta Hedman 2–1 in the final at Lakeside.

No sooner had Anastasia secured her second World Championship than the *Sun* newspaper reported that Anastasia 'could quit' the BDO after officials apparently tried to ban her dart flights just thirty minutes before her semi-final match against Trina Gulliver.

Anastasia commented, 'About my flights it's true. It was about twenty minutes before the game and a minute before I was bulling up with Trina.'

It seems that, at the time of writing, any possible threat to defect again has dissipated as a spokesman said that Anastasia has no plans other than to defend her BDO title

TOPLESS DARTS

As if darts didn't have enough trouble fighting against those who branded it a pub game trying to be a sport featuring unfit men with huge bellies who swilled copious pints of lager from dawn 'til dusk, the last thing it really wanted was any suggestion that nudity could be associated with the sport. However, it seems unbelievable that topless models, a nude dart player, a streaker and a 'topless' darts celebration would bring further, perhaps unwanted, attention to the sport.

L!VE TV

In January 1996 Kelvin MacKenzie, managing director of the tabloid cable channel *L!ve TV*, announced the new schedule which included half-naked young ladies apparently throwing darts. The initial venue for production was Australia's Bondi Beach where a colleague of Mackenzie's was told to find 'girl-next-door types, but with nice tits.'

In December 1995, *Private Eye* confirmed the completion of the filming of *Topless Darts* commenting, 'Unfortunately the games will lack any sporting integrity: the topless women were so crap at darts that they will only be seen launching the arrows.'

The BDO was quoted as condemning the show as 'demeaning to [the] sport as well as potentially dangerous to participants' but they need not have worried about the latter. The girls were filmed tossing a coin, jumping about and even mouthing 'I won! I won!' but they never threw a dart at the board. The darts were thrown by members of the production team one of whom said that *Topless Darts* was good, clean 'saucy' fun.

As for Kelvin MacKenzie, in a letter in December 1995 he wrote that '*Topless Darts* is simply a piece of fun which is not in any way designed to upset the punters.'

NAKED DARTER

Dutch lady darts player Mieke de Boer (nicknamed 'Bambi') who reached the semi-finals of the Lakeside Ladies' World Darts Championship in 2003 was the first and only (so far) female darter to feature in *Playboy* magazine.

TOPLESS (WELL NAKED ACTUALLY AT THE) DARTS

Streaking (the art of stripping off (either planned or spontaneous) and running amok anywhere one fancies) was a fad in the 1970s which still occurs today. Rugby, cricket, snooker and other sports all witnessed male and/or female streakers during a main event but darts fans had to wait until the 2000s to witness the sport's first streaker at a major tournament. It occurred at Lakeside in the 2001 Embassy World Professional Darts Championship; the first streaker in over twenty years of televised darts.

Emma Hughes, a 24-year old hairdresser from Oxford, stripped off and ran across the stage during the first round match between Ted Hankey and Shaun Greatbatch. Emma certainly impressed the male darts fans but officials were very concerned and the young lady was soon covered up and led away.

MC and referee Martin Fitzmaurice named Emma's streak as his only disappointment in twenty years of involvement with the tournament. He said, 'I was sitting out the back when the streaker came on, so I didn't see it.' However, a short time later, Martin did step out on to the Lakeside stage and told the crowd, 'The streaker will be heavily fined for not wearing an official badge on stage.'

When asked for his comments, Bobby George is quoted as replying, 'I've seen some good double tops up on that stage, but never anything like that!'

Although Emma's dash was originally expected to be featured in the two-video box set *The Story of Darts,* for whatever reason she was left on the cutting room floor. However, Emma later appeared on the Dutch darts DVD *Let's Play Darts.*

Just in case you're curious, Ted Hankey beat Shaun Greatbatch 3–0.

CALENDAR GIRLS –
DARTS STYLE

When it came to deciding how they could raise hundreds of pounds for the Hull-based Dove House Hospice, a team of lady darters took inspiration from the film *Calendar Girls* and bared all in 2007 for a calendar for the following year.

Titled the Hull Darts Calendar Girls 2008 the ladies posed naked for the camera, their positions, all pub-related, included playing cribbage – Jenny and Kath (June), holding a large plate of sandwiches was Cheryl (July), playing pool was Jenny (October) and a number of darts-related shots. Local firms and businesses sponsored per calendar month.

Co-organiser Dave Taylor said, 'The girls loved taking part in the project for such a good cause.'

TOPLESS DARTS CELEBRATION

When the 12-strong Top Bull pub darts team from Breightmet, Bolton, won the Bury and District Darts League in the early 1990s, they hired an open-top, 'topless' double-decker bus for two hours the following Sunday to celebrate. Bedecked with ribbons and bunting, the bus carried the victorious team – cup held aloft – through the local streets.

Pub landlord and team player Dave Cubbin is reported to have said, 'Manchester United had an open-top bus to mark winning the Premier [English football] League and so did Bolton Wanderers when they clinched promotion to Division One. We reckon our victory is just as great a sporting triumph!'

Dave's wife Jan then revealed one of the secret weapons in the Top Bull's team armoury. His name was Jimmy Ferrymound – aged 63. Jan told a reporter, 'His secret is in his pipe. He keeps it in his mouth when he throws his arrows.'

ORGANISATIONAL CHANGE

After nearly a decade of development and rapid progress, the Professional Darts Corporation, established in 1992, had succeeded in totally changing the image and direction of the sport of darts. That change was then to accelerate when on 26 July 2001 a fax to all sports editors announced that 'Barry Hearn has accepted an invitation to become Chairman of the PDC.'

In the subsequent press conference and photocall held at 11.00 a.m. at the Imperial Hotel, Blackpool, on Monday 30 July 53-year-old Hearn, who was also in Blackpool to attend the Stan James World Matchplay Championship and who had already played a major role in turning snooker into a multi-million pound global sport, promised to achieve the same level of success for darts. His credentials in relation to sports management were second to none having in the past managed snooker star Steve Davis and boxers including Nigel Benn and Chris Eubank. (Hearn was later to become Phil Taylor's manager.)

He enthused about the players, telling reporters, 'The current crop of top players in the PDC are genuine sports stars with unique ability. I intend to give them the profile they deserve to turn them into superstars,' adding, 'Phil Taylor is the closest any sport has to rivalling Tiger Woods.'

Rod Harrington, at that time the World no. 4, said, 'Barry Hearn will give the sport great credibility and will help to get the professionals established.'

THE NEW BOY

At the time of his appointment as Chairman of the PDC, Hearn said, 'Hopefully I can head up a team that can take darts on in the new millennium and to the level we all feel it should be. It's a sport that gets huge audiences everywhere it goes. Internationally its television exposure has been growing dramatically for the past six years. Domestically the audiences have really grown into substantial figures and so the platform is there to take it to the next level.'

Looking back after a mere eight months in the job, Hearn commented that it had been 'a hugely successful time' with the Skol

World Championship being 'quite simply the most prestigious world professional tournament darts has ever seen'; the icing on the cake being 'the decision of seven pros to defect to the PDC from the BDO' which he said showed 'how much confidence the top players have in the direction we are going.'

Defections continue to the present day.

Of his PDC colleagues, Hearn insisted that 'we mustn't let our standards slip if we hope to see the game achieve its full potential.'

INDECENT PROPOSAL?

The PDC under Hearn made immense progress during the following decade; the number of televised events increased and prize money rose from 'a minimum of £2 million on offer to players' in 2007 to a massive £5 million in 2010. But Barry Hearn had another target for the latter put of the first decade of the millennium; unification of the sport of darts under one umbrella organisation, the PDC.

In the December 2009 issue, *Darts World* revealed that the PDC had sent a letter to the BDO offering to purchase the organisation for £1 million and to pump a similar amount into the grass roots of the sport. Not exactly turning the offer down flat straight away, in January 2010 Olly Croft was quoted as saying, 'We want to know what's behind it before we can move forward but you won't get a decision overnight. Our property is worth more than what he's offered and we want to know what he wants to do with the second million pounds he's offered.' Two-time BDO World Champion Martin Adams told reporters, 'I don't want to play in the PDC. I've no interest in being one organisation. I want the BDO to remain as it is.'

Adams' wish was granted when on 31 January a very brief press release was issued by the BDO. Headed 'BDO REJECT OFFER', it read, 'At a full Council meeting attended by 65 counties on January 31st, 2010, a majority vote by county delegates instructed the BDO Board to reject an offer by the PDC to "buy" the BDO.'

On 4 February the PDC issued a statement in which Barry Hearn said that the Corporation was disappointed with the decision made by the BDO Board on two counts, 'Firstly we wanted a meeting with the member counties and clearly the majority did not want that meeting.

Secondly we wanted due diligence on their records. They did not want us to look at their books.'

Hearn added, 'When you look at their decision, it shows the ineptitude of the amateur game. For us at the PDC, it saves us £2 million which we can plough back into the development of our sport, but our door is always open to them.'

The BDO who viewed Hearn's offer as merely a 'gimmick' never set foot through that door again.

WHITHER THE £2M?

Later that same month the PDC announced 'new exciting plans' which it must be assumed had been part of the organisation's contingency plans formulated on the basis that the BDO would refuse the offer. These plans comprised the establishment of the PDC World Cup of Darts, the PDC Unicorn Under-21 World Championship and the PDC Unicorn Women's World Championship.

As far as the Grand Slam of Darts (GSD) (established in 2007) was concerned, the finalists of the PDC Unicorn Under-21 and Women's World Championships would be invited to compete in the GSD in November 2010 and invitations previously issued to the BDO Lakeside Women's World Professional Darts Championship and the Winmau World Masters would be withdrawn, although the four invitations from the men's Lakeside World Professional Darts Championship would continue to apply.

Controversially, with regard to the World Masters, the statement issued by the PDC stated, 'The PDC feels that with eight players seeded through to the final stages and a level of prize money below standard PDC ProTour Weekends the Winmau World Masters does not reach credible qualification criteria.'

With regard to the PDC ProTour Cards, in addition to the automatic granting of Tour Cards for the finalists of the PDC Unicorn Under-21 and Women's World Championship events, the PDC would be granting card membership to the four semi-finalists of the BDO Lakeside World Championship 'on application'.

Finally, as a way of thanking the eight counties who voted in favour of 'at least discussing the PDC's offer to the BDO', the PDC offered each of those one spot in the 2010 PDC UK Open, 'with the qualification criteria to be discussed individually with each relevant county.'

Barry Hearn reinforced his message that 'The aim of our offer to the BDO was to unify the sport of darts and this remains our long-term objective despite the decision of the BDO County Associations,' adding, 'We shall continue to drive this great sport forward undismayed by the intransigencies of the amateur game which is built on inept financial management, self-interest and mediocrity."

ALL CHANGE AT THE BDO

Towards the end of 2010 there was talk of dissension in the ranks of the BDO, that there were moves afoot to oust the 'old stagers' from control of the organisation. By early 2011 much work was going on behind the scenes and within a few short months Olly Croft and most of his fellow elder statesmen of the BDO, the cement that had held that darts code together for 38 years, were voted off at a meeting of BDO counties in Coventry in August. Of the outgoing board only Vic Sexton stayed on as 'Rules Director' while the highly respected Sam Hawkins was made Honorary President of the BDO, a title and position well-deserved given his lifetime commitment to darts and the BDO.

A 'new' BDO board emerged headed by Essex County Darts Chairman Barry Gilbey and including three-time world darts champion Martin Adams in the post of 'Players Director'. Although Olly realised that something was afoot he had no idea that the BDO which he and his colleagues had nurtured for so many years would be so completely and utterly wrested from their control in what has been described as a 'coup'. Olly is now writing his autobiography which should make interesting reading. One chapter is tentatively titled 'TREASON!' a word that simply summarises his feelings of the events working up to August 2011.

The new BDO board has a wealth of invaluable knowledge and experience in darts that has been brought together for the very first time. The new board described itself as 'progressive', with its aims and aspirations 'firmly focussed on the BDO's important mission statement of "Darts For All" and the continuation of providing affordable and competitive darts and opportunities for all players, irrespective of age, gender or ability.'

In the programme notes of the 2012 Lakeside World Professional Darts Championship, the new Chairman, Barry Gilbey told fans, 'We are extremely confident and excited about our future objectives and initiatives on behalf of our players and officials. Everyone on the new board has experience and skills in their individual roles, and I guarantee that all of our planned changes going forward will be made to improve and benefit everyone within the BDO.'

'Darts for All' continues to be the key aim of the revitalised BDO and, as far as a strategy for the future is concerned, a consultation document was sent out to the WDF as well as all member countries and many players. The document outlined the plans for the Invitation Tables which feed into the Lakeside World Professional Darts Championship.

So there currently remain two organisations controlling their specific elements of the sport of darts and it seems that never the twain shall meet, except, of course, when players from both codes contest the Grand Slam of Darts.

HOW TO ACHIEVE THE PERFECT GAME

As top darters continue to hit perfect games of 501 on a regular basis, achieving a nine-darter becomes the standard expectation of darts fans attending major tournaments and they go away disappointed if one or more isn't produced.

John Lowe continues to travel the UK and the rest of the world playing exhibition matches and being part of the 'Legends' tours in front of ever-enthusiastic crowds, his Q & A sessions afterwards *always* include a question about that first televised nine-darter back in 1984; what John calls his 'Two and a half minutes of perfection'.

Despite many others subsequently equalling John's feat (but not all achieving his £102,000 pay day) the acclaim for that first televised perfect game has followed John around the globe for more than twenty-five years.

The questions are usually about how he felt and how much he paid in tax but occasionally he is asked 'What is the secret of hitting a nine-darter?' For all those who want to try to emulate John, here he reveals the path to adopt to have the very best chance of hitting that perfect 501.

The secret is out.
Here are the fascinating facts on how to hit a nine-darter.

- Ensure that you are prepared both mentally and physically as you would do for every match you play.

- Check that you have the right equipment; that your darts and flights are in pristine condition.

- Ensure that the equipment (the dartboard, the oche, etc.) is set up correctly.

- Play the game as you would in any other serious darts tournament.

- Make sure you are ready when the moment arrives. (A true professional will *always* be ready.)

- Carefully negotiate the penultimate challenge of your skills; the odd-numbered treble.

- Cross the finishing line by hitting that double with precision.

- Afterwards share your success with those who have supported you for a long time; those who care about you.

That's all there is to it! (Thanks John.)

Before we leave nine-darters, those who strive to achieve Nirvana will be thrilled to learn that Bobby George has worked out that there are no less than 145 combinations and an amazing total of 3,944 sequences that you can go for. Surely that makes the task a bit easier!

DR DARTS ON CREATING A DARTS MYTH

Earlier in this book it was revealed that a number of stories relating to the sport of darts were accepted for many years as fact but are actually products of the fertile minds of either pranksters or the misinformed. The 'hockey' being named after a West Country brewer has been shown to be one of the most popular of these myths while the 'Bigfoot' Annakin court has been proven to be true but over time has become a victim of journalistic exaggeration.

Unfortunately, sitting back in the reflected glory and self-satisfaction of debunking myths can lead to complacency. So here's where it went wrong.

APRIL FOOLISHNESS

Everyone likes to have a laugh and in the late 1990s and early 2000s I was asked by the then Press Officer of the PDC to produce a piece of tomfoolery for 1 April; a darts April Fool.

These hoaxes were also featured on my website www.patrickchaplin. com. When this annual foolishness was no longer required by the PDC I continued to write them for my website and, since 2010, for my *Dr Darts' Newsletter* (*DDN*).

In 2008, in *DDN*, I featured an article about the totally fictitious Fal Priolo, a 24-year-old Guatemalan darts ace who had arrived in the UK for his first darts tour of Britain and lost his luggage at the new Heathrow Terminal Five building. Fal had told waiting reporters, 'I am very much looking forward to licking your Phil Taylor. Bring on your "Crafty Cockey" and "Old Stonevoice" too. I am here to show the world that there is more to Guatemala than raising cattle and growing coffee.'

To my surprise, someone contacted me to say that he never realised that darts was played in Guatemala and asked for more details about Fal and his darts career.

But it was an article written initially for the PDC and published on their website on 1 April 2002 that will live long in my memory. The piece, which was eventually transferred to my website, was titled 'Is this the Oldest Oche?' and was a contrived story about an ancient seventeenth-century oche being discovered walled up in an old Essex pub, the Magpie, during major renovations to the building. The claim was that this surely must be the oldest oche extant in the UK or anywhere else for that matter.

Since then I occasionally receive enquiries asking if the story is true. Of course, I tell them that it is pure fabrication.

MYTH-MAKER

However, one researcher visited my website in search of the oldest oche and, not realising that it was a piece of April foolishness and with no reference to me, put it into print.

No lesser publication than the *Independent* magazine featured the information in an article entitled 'Minor British Institutions – Darts' stating that 'the "Oldest oche in the world" – dating back about 350 years – was uncovered in a former pub in Essex . . .'

Having spent more than thirty years researching darts, seeking out hundreds of fascinating facts and exploding myths and debunking legends about the sport of darts, it appears that I have now succeeded in creating a myth of my own!

Acknowledgements

T his book would not have been possible without the help and support of friends and family both within and without darts. In particular I would like to thank my wife Maureen, Dave Allen (Professional Darts Corporation), Colin Barrell, Lee Bennett (www. dartsmad.com), Dave Bevan, Vince Bluck (NODOR International), Karen Cookson (www.angelselite.co.uk), Mat Coward, Olly Croft CBE, Ian Flack (Winmau Dartboard Co.), Glen Huff, Thierry Gellinck, Bobby and Marie George, David King, Dave Lanning, John Lowe, Edward Lowy (Unicorn Products), Chris Murray, Dan William Peek, Robert Pringle (Harrows Darts Technology), Colin Saunders, Andrew C. Scott (Professional Darts Players' Association), Judy Sharp, Michelle Tilling and her colleagues at The History Press, the late Sid Waddell, and Tony Wood, editor of *Darts World* (1972–2009).

About the Author

Patrick Chaplin has been researching and writing about darts for more than 25 years and playing darts (in his fashion) for longer than he cares to remember.

Winner of a few pub-level darts trophies, Patrick began delving into darts history in the mid-1980s when, in a local pub his best friend asked, 'What's the true history of darts then Pat?' Patrick said he would let him know in a fortnight.

That was back in the summer of 1985 . . .

In 2006 Patrick was awarded a PhD for his dissertation *Darts in England 1900–1939: A Social History.* Author of several books on darts, including collaborations with Bobby George, Trina Gulliver and John Lowe, Patrick is the only person on the planet to have obtained a PhD in the social history of darts, a fascinating fact that led to him being dubbed 'Dr Darts' by the tabloid press – a soubriquet that suits him fine. He also has an authoritative website and produces his monthly *Dr Darts' Newsletter* which has subscribers from around the globe. Patrick is also an Honorary Visiting Research Fellow in History, Anglia Ruskin University, Cambridge.

He lives in Essex with his wife Maureen.

Author's other Publications and Website

PUBLICATIONS
Sole author
The Official Bar Guide to Darts (Puzzlewright Press, New York, 2010)
Darts in England 1900-1939 – A social history (Manchester University
    Press, 2009)

Collaborations
With John Lowe
Old Stoneface – The Autobiography of Britain's Greatest Darts Player
    (John Blake, London, 2005 (updated, revised paperback 2009))
The Art of Darts (Hodder & Stoughton, London, 2009)

With Trina Gulliver
Golden Girl – The Autobiography of the Greatest Ever Ladies' Darts Player
    (John Blake, London, 2008)

With Bobby George
Scoring for Show, Doubles for Dough – Bobby George's Darts Lingo
    (Apex Publishing, Clacton-on-Sea, 2011)

NEWSLETTER
Anyone can subscribe to *Dr Darts' Newsletter*, a monthly online
publication keeping fans up to date with Patrick's current research and
other items of general interest from across the world. Simply send an
e-mail to info@patrickchaplin.com and sign up.

WEBSITE
www.patrickchaplin.com